On the Steps

Copyright © Shameka M Staley
Edited by: Kelli L Cofield
Revised and Contributions by: Tangenik Phya Webb
Cover design by: Elexus D Dorsey
All rights reserved.

ISBN: 1490427562
ISBN-13: 9781490427560

On the Steps

Shameka M Staley

*To: Danette Powell
Thank you so much for your support. I pray that you will be inspired by this book.
Peace & Blessings
S. [signature]
2014*

What is the book about? It is an autobiography, a non-fiction short story, a miniature version of the life I live from past to present. This non-fiction work of art is full of memories, experiences, facts, and imaginable moments of the untold truth.

Targeted audience? My targeted audience: teenagers and young adults, particularly ages 16-35.

Purpose: My purpose for writing this autobiography is to inspire, motivate, and encourage those who may have been faced with similar situations. Writing this book doesn't provide direct answers, but it does provide truth, through personal experience, emotions, feelings, spiritual guidance and acceptance. Writing this book was like therapy to my soul and it forced me to dig deep into the dark side of life many like to keep a secret.

My Life: I honestly believe that my life is a living testimony designed to help others. My life is a witness to those who fail to remember their own wrongdoing and to those who live life through their own vision of perfection. My life is a test of faith, a test of accepting, understanding and finding ways to look past the death sentence of man's judgment. I am learning to embrace my gifts and ability to touch and change lives.

Dedication: I dedicate this book to my Lord and Savior, my Creator who is gracefully allowing me to live through this term called life. I also dedicate this book to my mother, who embraced and nurtured me since birth. I love you Mommy and lastly, I dedicate this book to every individual that is or has gone through life-changing experiences. I pray that my life and this book will be used as a testimony to many.

Acknowledgments

Special thanks to all of those who believed writing this book was a possibility. I appreciate those who supported me when I experienced personal and financial hardships. I want to also thank those who encouraged me to strive harder in what I believed in and those who dissuaded me when I wanted to quit. Every individual that I have come in contact with thus far has played a tremendous part in both my life and writing. There are some that have had a bigger influence, but whether big or small, I credit all of you for helping me become who I am today and I am forever grateful.

I want to thank my mother (Jeanette Bell), who has always been there for me throughout everything. She has taught me that every good thing comes from God and all of which he has and will give me, I vow to her.

I am eternally grateful for my father (Mervin Bell), brothers (Eric, Mervin Jr., and Mark Bell), sisters-in-law (Madeca & Yolonda Bell), nieces and nephews (Te'asha, Little Marc, Irvin, E.J, Mylz, Madison, Meagon, M.J, Savannah and Mason). I send a special thanks to my grandparents (the late Voncile Kinard and Carolee Bell), aunts, cousins, uncles, and biological family, especially my biological father (John Bowman). Our relationship is growing daily. The love and support of my family has outweighed the bad days.

I would like to say thank you to all of my wonderful friends who have stuck by me and encouraged me over the years. There are too many of you to name, but know that I am forever indebted to you and I thank you for your friendship. However there is one that I must mention, Latasha Kearise. You have shared every day with me for the last eight years. You have supported and encouraged me unbeknownst to many. I have grown to gain an even greater love for you through our differences, laughter, honesty and tears. You are the greatest roommate one could ever have. You have lent your shoulder to my tears, an ear to my pains and have carried me more times than not. You are truly a blessing and I love you.

Lastly, I want to thank those who have pushed me closer to God: Pastor Gathers

(Life Cathedral - my home church in South Carolina), Elder Fowlkes (Kingdom Builders C.O.G.I.C – Hanover, Maryland), and Bishop Ralph and Gregory Dentist (Kingdom Worship Center – Baltimore, Maryland). Your ministries and your leadership have blessed my soul tremendously. I know that you all will continue to be blessed for all that you do for your congregation and me.

Contents

STEP 1: The Creation of a Baby Girl   1

STEP 2: A Woman's Prayer Comes True   5

STEP 3: A Story That Tells It All   9

STEP 4: Lost & Confused   15

STEP 5: Finding My Way Back to God's House   21

STEP 6: A New Outlook on Life   27

STEP 7: Finding My Biological Father   35

STEP 8: Transition   49

STEP 9: The Beginning of a New Journey   57

STEP 10: In Search of my Purpose While On This Journey   75

STEP 11: The Pressure of the Process   83

Introduction

I had no idea that my past was haunting me. For the past 20 years, I was ignorant to the effects of it. I not only had problems with my past, but also with my present. I was used to pointing fingers, complaining, hurting, and running. I did so until I would completely lose track of the initial problem. Physically, I have managed to push myself through life. I have struggled emotionally and mentally, I programmed myself to keep moving forward, no matter what. Some people may question what is wrong with pushing yourself forward if you're doing good things in life. I would have agreed with that very sentiment before writing this book.

In October 2003, shortly after graduating from Claflin University, a historically black college in my hometown of Orangeburg, South Carolina, I made a big move. I was almost forced to relocate after graduating from college. Things took a huge turn and I had to get started with my new journey. I had no idea what I was walking into, but man was I in for a surprise. During the end of October, I made my first big move to Baltimore, Maryland, a place where I had no family, just one friend from college and my oldest brother's best friend. Making that unexpected move to Baltimore was when my life unfolded from past to present. My major in college was sociology so I managed to find a job within the human services field with no problem. I was working with children, teenagers, and young adults who faced being abused and neglected, physically, mentally, verbally, and emotionally. Some of them had been abandoned and left alone in the middle of the night. Most of them just wanted to catch a break. Some of them wanted sympathy, while others just wanted someone to listen, love and to be shown attention. I would listen to them complain about their circumstances, realizing that they all had their own way of dealing and coping with each situation. Whether it was acting out physically, being mentally distressed or emotionally frustrated, I had never seen anything like it. For some reason, they showed me respect and enjoyed being in my presence. It was almost like they knew or saw something in me that I didn't even see in myself. After a while I started noticing my past slowly begin to haunt me. Something had to be done about my past creeping into my present. The more I lived and worked with different people in Baltimore, the more I started seeing things in me I never knew were there.

Life does not stop because we feel like we were dealt a bad hand or because our situations seem unfair. We get so caught up in pointing fingers, complaining, and running that we never stop to think about what is really the problem. God laid it on my heart to write about my story not for sympathy, but for reality, strength, motivation, inspiration, and hope. Through my writing I am not only writing to others, but I am ministering to myself. I am also gaining trust, faith, commitment, and guidance within God. Physically, I still push myself forward; emotionally, I am facing my situations head on; and mentally, I am growing each and every day of my life. Please use this as a stepping-stone toward facing your past and present situations realizing that you can and will survive if you trust in God and believe in yourself. By no means am I saying that reading this book, trusting God, and believing in yourself will stop the trials of life, but it does allow you to sustain. As for me, I hope to experience strength, peace, joy, patience, and forgiveness, among other things. Walk with me through this journey of my life as it unfolds from beginning to the present. Listen to the words, embrace the experience, and take in the laughter. Visualize the steps, feel the pain, and together we can expect to gain all that God has for us.

Listen

I write from a self-point of view.
But don't get it confused, this is a true story.
Close up view of my journey.
Destined to gain purpose you see.

Giving back to the community,
Fighting my struggles to keep my dignity,
Twenty-eight with a vision
Trying hard to pave the way at least that's what they say

The building of a kingdom
A kingdom of development I am seeking
A chance to provide structure
Bring back respect
Acknowledge He who created me

The children are the future
Who holds the key?
Guiding us through what life will be
Praying daily for peace of mind
Strength in youth bodies
Spirit in their souls
Reaching out, picking up where we left off

Dreaming of what the world could be
Leaving behind poverty, hypocrites
Unbalanced democracy
Allowing division in society
With a lack of growth and development
If only someone would stop and listen.

Step 1: The Creation Of A Baby Girl

Everyday all over the world a child is being born. Some are born premature, some die at birth, some turn out extremely healthy, and some turn out abandoned. Then there's me, who was forsaken, but still blessed. So many women are having children, but battle with making a decision that best suits the child's well-being. Trying to understand the inner feelings of a woman giving birth is hard to determine when she is faced with abuse, drugs, and stress. Who knows what is in the mind of women who neglect or abuse their children. Every child has a right to be given the opportunity to eventually be unwrapped, nurtured and developed into the design he or she was destined to be. However situations sometimes arise causing a change in direction or even a scar on one's heart forever, but in God, I trust and pray that eyes will open, hearts will forgive, and the mind will understand that our creation was not an accident.

According to Rick Warren, you are not an accident! Your birth was no mistake or mishap and your life is no fluke of nature. Your parents may not have planned you, but God did. He was not at all surprised by your birth. In fact, He expected it. Long before your parents conceived you, you were conceived in the mind of God. He thought of you first. It is not fate, nor chance, nor luck, nor coincidence that you are breathing at this very moment. You are alive because God wanted to create you (Warren, 2002)!

Of course this all seems true, but as a child growing up, suffering from neglect, abandonment, and many other issues, they don't really understand the words of Rick Warren. They only want to know why, how, and when is it going to get better again. It takes time, prayer, help, hope, and maybe even years, but one day the words of Rick Warren will come to pass and save a soul lost from within. Step by step the life of a child unfolds and only God can direct the path of destination through whom He has created.

On January 6, 1980 in Orangeburg, South Carolina, the creation of a beautiful baby girl was brought into this world. I had no idea of what life was or could ever be. The only thing I could feel was racing heartbeats and bright lights beaming on my soft skin. Never imagining the woman giving birth could be so overwhelmed with abuse and drug habits that she would have thoughts of giving me, her precious child, away. The woman closed her eyes tightly as she began to ask God for help.

Dear God please help me. I have been down this road twice already, making this my third time and once again I am unable to care for my child. I love my children, but God the life they deserve is a life I can't give at this time, she prayed. Thinking back to when she gave her other two children away tears, started to roll down her face. As the tears dropped, the doors of the hospital room opened and the nurses entered taking me away to clean off what could possibly be the last scent of my mother. I was never given a chance to be embraced by her love or a minute to smile in her face. The nurses came in and changed up the pace.

Alright Misses Staley, it is time for us to clean her up.

Please, please just give me one more second.

One second, that's all we can give you, at least until we get her cleaned up. We will be sure to bring her right back.

The second was up and the nurse walked out of the room holding me tightly in her arms. The doors closed and my birth mother starts to think back when she gave her first two children to family members hoping she could do the same for me, her new baby girl.

A week of pacing and decision-making was quickly approaching and something had to be done. Thoughts of my birth mother giving her first two children away started to cross her mind once again as she continued to pace back and forth. My oldest sister lived with her paternal grandmother and my older brother lived with his maternal grandmother. Even though they were separated, they were still close to one another. My birth mother started thinking to herself what her life would be like if she kept me tagging along while dealing with abuse from her companion at the time. Struggling with abuse, being young, and moving around from place to place was starting to make her realize that I would be better off with someone else. She battled with whom she knew that could provide love, shelter, support, and strength in my life. The night continued with my birth mother tossing and turning, contemplating on all the possible outcomes. The possibility of her finding a family who could take care of me was taking over her mind. Tears began to drop as my birth mother caught flash backs of being beaten over and over again. Her abusive relationship played a huge part in her not being able to take care of me. I guess she was in something she couldn't get out of, or maybe she just didn't have what it took at the time to raise a child.

What are you doing? Stop it! Stop it!

Don't tell me what to do. I am the man of the house and you will do what I say, and when I say it. Let's not have this conversation again. Is that understood?

Quickly snapping out of the daze, she picked me up, closed her eyes and waited until dawn. I imagine that she felt a connection when she picked me up, but it proved to be a fleeing moment. Two nights in the hospital and it was time for us to leave. We went back to my birth mother's home, but not for long. It only took a few more nights of pacing, tossing and turning for the bad dreams to come to an end.

Step 2: A Woman's Dream Comes True

On the other side of town, we have a married couple that gave birth to three boys hoping and praying for a little girl. This woman knew her medical situation would not allow her to have any more children, but she continued to pray, asking God for that special gift. The woman dreamt about what it would be like to have a daughter to hold tight in her arms, showing her what it felt like to be loved. The woman would always stand in the kitchen by the window praying that the impossible would someday exist. This family attended church and prayed together, but something was still missing. One day she had been preparing breakfast for her family standing in her favorite spot by the window and her husband walked over and said,

Hey! Baby are you alright

Ahh ya ya! Just thinking.

Are you sure?

As tears began to roll down her face, she yearned, "baby you know how much I wanted a baby girl. I mean I love my boys so much, but I can't help but think about what it would have been like to have a little girl".

"I know, I know. You are not alone. Remember, it's not over just yet. Keep praying baby, just keep praying," spoke her husband while joining her in tears.

I don't know, maybe it is over.

The woman began to voice the impossible out loud crying and hoping for an answer. Thinking back to her history of being sick, the woman closed her eyes repeating to herself the simple wish of a baby girl. "A baby girl is all I ask."

God allowed the possible for one woman to connect with the impossible of another, using the power of their tongues to create a miracle. A knock at the door broke the woman and her husband out of their conversation. She dried her eyes as she approached the door. Her hands slipped of the doorknob as they were still damp from wiping away tears. Looking down on the step she noticed a small beautiful baby girl only two weeks old sitting in a carrier waiting to be held tight in someone's arm.

"Hello", the woman said "how are you doing, may I help you?"

"I am doing alright", said Misses Staley.

Wow! She's beautiful and why do you have her out this early? Well huh! Well huh; not giving misses Staley time to answer.

The woman invited my birth mother and me in and they began to talk. The two women knew each other for years because the woman's husband was a first cousin with my birth mother. My birth mother knew the woman wanted a little girl but due to medical reasons she was unable to have any more children.

My birth mother sat down on the chair and began to cry out for help. Opening up to the woman she explains her abusive relationship and inability to take care of any children at the time. I guess she got tired of tossing, pacing, and fighting in her sleep.

You see I have been back and forth with him and things are only getting worse. I love my kids, but I just can't care for them."

Why does he beat you like that?

I don't know. He comes home upset all the time and I just don't know how to control him anymore. He drinks so much and the drugs are taking over his mind.

Well, what about you? Are you using drugs and drinking?

I mean, I mean I am trying my best to do the right thing but it's not easy you know. I just can't walk away like that. I mean he loves me you know. He wants a family and all that stuff, but I guess it's not a good time for him since he got laid off and all.

So tell me what are you going to do?

Well that's why I am here. I was wondering if you and Mervin could watch her for a little while at least until I could get myself together.

Until you can get yourself together huh!

Yea, it'll only be for about two weeks, I promise. I mean he should be working by then and things should be a little better with us you know.

The woman looks down at me while I am smiling showing multiple signs of wanting to be loved. Thinking to herself how wonderful it would be to have a baby girl, the woman said, 'I need to talk it over with my husband first'. My birth mother understood, but hoped that the woman would ask her husband immediately. "Well I guess I'll ask him now since I see you are in a rush". "Oh well yes just a little bit I gotta get back home you know. He is waiting on me". The woman proceeded to beckon her husband.

"Hey! Baby can you come in here for a minute" said the woman.

"Hey! What's going on, said Mervin.

"Hello Mervin, how are you doing?"

"I am fine. Can someone tell me what's going on please?"

"Yes. I have to ask if you and Jeanette could watch my baby girl for a little while at least until I can get myself together. I have been dealing with a lot and at this time I don't think I can give her the love and care she needs."

"What about Ross and Tam, your other two kids", asked Mervin.

"Well Ross is with my mother, your aunt and Tam is with her father's mother, but they are both close to one another. I had them with me for a while but things started getting out of control in my life once again so I had to do what was best for my kids. I love my kids and I pray God will keep them safe. I will get it right. I just need a little time that's all."

"Well..." said Mervin while looking down at the beautiful baby girl, "I am ok with it. How can anyone resist taking in such a beautiful gift? What is her name?"

"Well uh! You see I made a small mistake with the spelling of her name and didn't have a chance to get it straight you know."

"Well what is it?"

"I was trying to spell Temika but instead it's Temerk."

"How could you do something like that, I mean what was on your mind at the time? I tell you what we are going to call her..."

Before Marvin could utter another word, his wife shouted, "Shameka that's what we will call her."

Ms. Staley insisted that that the new name was fine. She went on to offer thanks and promises to come back soon. She looked at me once more and then to Jeannette and told her of how she knew I was in great hands and gave another promise to come back soon. "I know things are going to get better. You know I just need to make it right with him."

"What about making it right with yourself and your children said Jeanette".

"Oh! Yes, yes, I am going to do that. I just need to get it right you know. God blessed me with you guys and I will forever be grateful to you two. She then got up and walked out the door.

Jeannette started to cry, not believing what had just happened. What she had been praying for was finally coming true. She had been hoping for a baby girl and now she had one to love and nurture. At that moment, Jeannette became my mother. She picked me up and held me tight. It was as if at the moment that we connected. While embracing me, my new parents gave thanks to God and glorified Him for this gift from heaven. My new father called the boys into the room to let them know what was going on.

"Hey! Boys, she will be staying with us for a while so let's make room for her.

"Wow! I always wanted a little sister and I finally got one said Anthony.

My older two brothers just watched me as I made small noises as if I could feel the love in the air. At the time I didn't know exactly what was going on, but I know that I enjoyed the feeling.

My mother snuck away for a quick second to pray, asking God for strength to care for me. While praying thoughts of Ms. Staley coming back to take me away crossed her mind. She immediately broke down into tears. My father walked into the room and notices her UN easiness, then reassured her of his beliefs that I would be with them longer than a few weeks. "God will see that she stays with us" he said.

Step 3: A Story That Tells It All

Two weeks turned into years and I was not a baby girl anymore. I guess my father was right about having me longer than a few weeks because I was now eight years old. As my mother looked down at me while I was playing, tears started to come down her face. I looked up at her and wondered why she was crying, but I never asked.

The phone rang breaking my mother's deep concentration. She proceeded to answer the phone. "Hello." A very unfamiliar voice was on the other end. "Who is this", asked my mother.

"This is me, Ms. Staley."

"Oh how are you doing?"

"Well things are getting a little better for me. I was able to get out of that bad relationship, but I got a new guy I am seeing now and he cares about me."

"Oh ok. So tell me what brings you back around after all these years? It seems like a few days turned into a few years. Don't get me wrong. My husband and I are not complaining at all, but do you realize what it does to this child?"

"What do you mean, I am her mother."

"Yes you are partly right, you are her birth mother. All these years we never knew when or if you would ever come back around. I never mentioned to Shameka the situation because I was still trying to wait until she was old enough."

"Well, well I want to come and see her if that's alright with you."

"I understand you would like to see her, but you will need to give us a little time to tell her about you."

"I don't see why we have to wait so long. I mean I am actually turning into the yard as we speak."

My mother hung up the phone shaking trying to make sure everything in the house was clean before my Ms. Staley got out of the car. While cleaning my father walked in the house and noticed a difference in my mother's facial expression. He asked about her change in mood as there was a knock on the door. My father walked over to open the door with a surprise look on his face. "Well look what the wind blew in after all these years", my mother said, giving my father a chance to get over his shock. Ms. Staley walked in and sat down right next to me. I was looking a little puzzled trying to figure out why that lady was staring at me like that. My mother told me to go outside and play for a little while.

Amazed at how beautiful I was; my birth mother watched me as I skipped my way outside. "Wow! I can't wait to tell everyone how beautiful she is", my birth mother said. "I see you guys have done a wonderful job with her, she is very beautiful. I mean she should be about eight by now if I am not mistaking." "Yes that's right. She is eight years old", my mother said. "Well I guess we have a lot of catching up to do", Ms. Staley said.

"Yes you are right. We have a lot of questions for you as well"

"What type of questions?"

"Well for starters, who and where is the child's father?"

"Well when I was pregnant with her I was dating two guys at the time and her father who is also my son's father didn't know she was his. During the time she was born I was already suffering from hurt and abuse so I had to make my companion at the time think the child was his. I mean if he knew I was cheating on him who knows what would have happened to my baby or me. After I told her real father she wasn't his child I haven't heard from him since."

"Did you ever think about what type of effect this can have on the child?"

"No! I was so busy thinking about myself. I forgot about the hurt I caused others. I knew my situation was messed up, but at least I tried to get my kids somewhere safe. I hoped one day I would be able to set the record straight with her father because she deserves the right to know about him and he deserves the right to know about her."

"Yes you're right about that. I mean I don't think you understand the hurt you have caused this child. The bad part about it is that we haven't even mentioned it to her," my father chimed in. "We were so busy trying to find the right time and even the words in which she would be able to understand."

"Yes I guess it might be a little hard but enough about that", Ms. Staley said. "Let's talk about why I am here. Over the past eight years or so many things has changed in my life and I want to make it up to all my kids."

"What are you trying to say", asked my mother.

"Well I would like to first thank you for everything, but I want to take my daughter with me."

My mother closed the door and sat down beside my father. "Ever since I can remember, I prayed for a daughter and God blessed me with a beautiful baby girl whom we have had for eight years. You came to us eight years ago and asked if we could take her in for a little while. Well as you can see, it's been more than just a little while. We have done just that, taken her in and cared for her as if she was our own. We never asked you for anything and now you are coming here wanting to take her away just like that. She is a part of us and without her our life would be incomplete."

Ms. Staley started to cry thinking back eight years ago on how she almost destroyed both my life and hers. She thought back to when she stayed up pacing the floor all night tossing, and fighting in her sleep. The room got quiet for a few minutes. Then my mother blurted out to Ms. Staley, "Do you honestly think you are capable of taking on the responsibility of raising this child?" Almost without thinking, Ms. Staley calmly admitted that she knew that she wasn't capable of taking care of a young child. "Then why take her away from a family who can and will provide her with what she needs?"

"I am just trying to do the right thing that's all."

"Believe it or not, you did the right thing eight years ago by bringing her here and you will be doing the right thing now by leaving her here with us", my mother said.

"I guess you are right. I just want my kids to know that I am their mother and I love them."

Sensing that Ms. Staley was genuinely concerned, my mom explained to her, "you can't take back what you have already done, but you can pick up from here and have a relationship with them.

"I want my baby to know about her biological family, so can you do me a favor and tell her about us, her biological family, including her father?

"That should not be a problem", my mother agreed, "but remember; we need to let her know about the situation before opening our doors for you to visit."

"I understand. Can I see her before I leave?

"Sure, I don't see any problem with that." My mother called me inside. As soon as I came in, I ran directly into my mother's arms. My mother stood back and said to me, "Meek say hello to Ms. Staley". I did as I was told, but still had a puzzled look on my face. I mean I never saw her around before so I was confused. The strange lady walked over to me and kneeled down, pinched my cheeks and kissed me on my head. I stepped back trying to figure out what was going on. I didn't understand because all she said to me after that was, "I'll see you soon". It all seemed weird to me so I said goodbye and went back outside. She thanked my parents again and then acknowledged the great job they've done. As she walked out, she said, "biologically I am the mother, but you have taken care of her and provided her with so much love. I don't know if I would have ever been able to give her that much love. Goodbye and see you soon." Just like that she walked away.

As soon as the strange lady left, I walked over to my mother and asked her, "Who was that lady kissing on me?" "Sit down baby, let's talk for a minute", my mom said patting the seat beside her. I was getting scared. I just wanted to know why that lady kissed me and I didn't even know her. She looked a little like me, but she couldn't be family because I had never seen her before. I went to sit down, but reminded my mother that this talk was going to shorten my outside time. She didn't pay me any attention and looked at me with a very serious face. When I noticed that my mother didn't crack a smile after that comment I knew this wasn't going to be an ordinary talk. Instead of sitting next to her, I pulled the kitchen chair up and sat right across from my mommy.

It seemed like my mother was having a hard time starting our conversation. She asked me a couple of random questions. It was almost like she wanted to make sure I would understand what she wanted to say.

It was somewhat strange because when she finally started the conversation she expressed how much she loved me. I started smiling saying I love you too, but she cut me off saying, "Please baby, I need for you to listen carefully to me". Everything she said to me afterwards was a huge shock. "Around the time you were born, a precious decision was made for your well-being. Soon after you were born, your birth mother decided that she couldn't take care of you." I jumped in and said, "Mom, what are you talking about? You are doing just fine taking care of me. She said, "Listen baby. The woman that was here earlier today is your birth mother. The best decision she made was allowing us to raise you. Every time I look at you, I think back to the day I opened the door and saw you sitting in your carrier on the steps waiting to be picked up. The smile on your face was so beautiful and it was at that moment I knew God had answered my prayers." I learned that my mother couldn't have any more children after she had my brothers because of an illness. I always knew my mom to be spiritual and she said that it was God who brought me to her. My mother said God had blessed her with me and she wanted me to know I will always be loved. She made sure I knew how much they all loved me and wanted me to be around for a very long time. She said she didn't tell me because she wanted to wait until I was old enough to understand. While my mother was talking I could tell she really meant every word and she felt bad about the situation. After she told me everything, I still didn't feel too bad. She was the only mom I ever knew and my brothers and my father was my family. I do think that I zoned out of the conversation at some point because I felt like I was dreaming. If I drifted off long enough maybe the dream would be over. When I tapped back in to the conversation, I realized it wasn't a dream.

Tears and questions started to pour out all at once. I had so many questions. "Do I have any other brothers or sisters? How did that lady find you? So who is my dad then? Is she going to take me away? Well it doesn't matter because I don't want to go anywhere and I am not leaving with her." I was so overwhelmed with feelings of hurt, anger, and confusion, but my mom answered every question one by one, never releasing me from her embrace.

"Yes you do have two other siblings. You have a brother named Ross and a sister named Tam."

"Where are they?"

"Well your brother lives with your biological grandmother and your sister lives with her father's mother."

"So I have a different father than my sister?"

"Yes, you and your brother have the same father but that doesn't mean that you two aren't still sisters."

"What about my father?"

"Well your father he, he, uh, uh… He still doesn't know about you just yet, but we are working on that."

"What do you mean he doesn't know about me?"

"Well your birth mother never had the chance to tell him that you were his child"

"So he doesn't know!!"

"Not yet baby, not yet."

"How did she find you and daddy?"

"Well she is actually your daddy's cousin so you see you were already related to us anyway."

My mom tried to explain to me that it didn't matter because she, my brothers and my father were my family. She told me that I could stay with them forever if I wanted to. I didn't even realize that I might have to leave them. She kept telling me that she loved me and I was her child. I don't know why, but she took up for my birth mother, telling me that she was sick and wasn't well enough to take care of me. She said it was a hard decision for my birth mother, but it was the right one. My mom always had a lesson involved and she told me that sometimes we have to do things we don't want to do, but there is a reason behind all things. After all of that, all I could do was asked my mom how she could allow this to happen to me.

With nothing else to say, I went from questioning my mother to questioning God. This just had to be His fault. I remember just crying myself to sleep that night. I didn't know what to expect and I just built a wall around myself. I knew it was nobody's fault but how could God put me through something like this? What did I do to deserve this? Why couldn't I have a normal family like everyone else? I had questions for days and needed answers fast. I was only eight years old, but was trying to understand things that I didn't even know existed. I never knew about parents giving their children away. I thought if you had children then you were supposed to raise them. All this time I thought my parents were my real parents. I knew I had a different last name, but I never thought to ask them about it. They never gave me reason to think I was not a part of their family, but how am I supposed to feel now?

Step 4: Lost And Confused

    Searching for answers to what seemed so confusing; I paced the floor day after day trying to put the pieces together. Thinking to myself what will my friends think about me? Does my family really love me even though I am not a part of their immediate family? I even thought and wondered what it would have been like living with my birth family? A knock at the door broke my thoughts as I wiped my eyes allowing the visitor to enter the room. It was my mother coming in to check on me. I immediately burst into tears all over again. My mother held me tight in her arms, but for some reason I rejected her. I guess it had a lot to do with me being confused. My mother didn't say much, but I could tell she felt my rejection and went directly into prayer.

    Dear God we need you right now! This child doesn't understand what is happening. Please reveal yourself. Give me the strength to continue providing and giving her the love she needs without her feeling like she's not wanted. In Jesus' matchless name, Amen!!

    After my mother finished praying, she asked me to tell her what was wrong. I refused to open up to her. I laid my head down on her shoulder as the tears rolled down my face. Deep down inside I felt heartbroken, hurt, untouched, useless, confused, scared, and somehow unloved, but it was too much to explain at the time. I could tell my mother had something else she wanted say, but needed a minute to say it. My mother moved over a bit so she could look me directly in the eyes. That's when I knew for sure she had something else she wanted to say. It was then that my mother told me how my birth family wanted to come and visit with me. This all seemed too sudden for me.

    Baby, I know this is hard for you right now so let's just take it one step at a time. I think you should know something. Before your birth mother left, she asked if she could come visit you soon.

    What did you say to her?

    Well I told her it would be up to you. Again I understand if you want to wait for a while.

    My mother told me that I didn't have to answer right away and to give it some thought. She also mentioned how visiting my birth family could be helpful. That seemed ridiculous to me at the time. How could she think I wanted to see someone that walked out on me? At that moment all I wanted to do was run away and hide underneath a rock. My mother got up and left the room. I guess it was to give me a little time to think about everything. I started to do just that, think. I began to think about how the initial conversation between my mother and my birth mother took place. I could only imagine that my mother was surprised and probably just responded with an 'Oh really'. What could she have said? "Could you watch my daughter for a few days?" I guess those few days turned into eight years. I can imagine being set down on the steps waiting for someone to pick me up. I mean what was so hard about her keeping me? After all she gave birth to me. I didn't ask to be brought into this world. Why should I give her a chance? She didn't give me one. Even though I felt so bitter, somehow I was a little curious about what my birth mother was like. I went back and forth in thought. One minute I was curious and the next minute I was upset about her walking out on me two weeks after I was born. It dawned on me that this was something I would deal with for the rest of my life.

A few weeks went by and I tried my best not to think about my situation, but it was a constant struggle and on my mind day and night. My birth mother called me a few times, but I had a hard time talking to her so I didn't. After a month or so I convinced myself that it wouldn't be that bad and had decided to call her. It was as if she knew that I was ready because the phone started ringing. It was her.

Hello can I speak to Meek?
This is her may I ask whose calling?
This is your birth mother, Ms. Staley.
Oh ok.
How have you been doing?
I am doing alright.
Well I was wondering if I could stop by and pick you up for some ice cream.
I guess that would be okay, but first I needed to ask my mother. Can you hold on for a minute? My mom said it was okay so I guess you can come after dinner.
Okay that sounds good. I will be there around 6:30pm.

I hung up the phone, walked into the living room and sat down on the couch. I looked up at the clock thinking to myself it's already 4:30pm. My birth mother will be here shortly. I could feel myself getting nervous by the second. I guess that's normal since I only know my family who I live with. I don't know this lady at all. I started imagining what the visit was going to be like, but of course my imagination was all over the place. Before I knew it dinner was over and it was 6:30pm. It was time for the visit I was waiting for and dreading at the same time. She came and picked me up and we went out for ice cream. The conversation was little to none because it seemed like neither one of us knew what to say. After ice cream she took me back home and asked my mother if she could come back in a few weeks to visit. Once she left, my mom sat down and started to talk to me.

How was the visit Meek?

It was alright. All we did was eat ice cream.

Well did she say anything else?

She just kept looking at me smiling. I didn't really know what that was about.

Well give her some time. She probably didn't know what to say. After all this is her first time with you since she gave birth to you. Is everything alright Meek?

Yes I am ok mom.

Well go ahead and get your things ready for school in the morning and I will check on you afterwards.

A few weeks passed by and it was time for another visit. It was like I counted down and dreaded the visits at the same time. I was nervous once again but it was too late to back out now, she was pulling up in the yard.

My birth mother was really excited when she came in. "Hey! How are you?"

I am ok.

You know I love you right Shameka? Oh ok. Well I do. So what are we going to do today? I thought we would go and visit your brother and sister if that's alright with you.

I guess that's alright.

As we rode off, I started imagining what this visit would be like. I didn't know how to talk to her. I mean should I call her mom, but I can't do that because I already have a mom. No, calling her mom was definitely out of the picture. I was so uncomfortable and confused but I tried my best not to let it show on my face. Once we arrived at the house I waited in the car. I was a little happy about having siblings though. I found it a little easier to relate and have conversations with my siblings than it was with my birth mother. I didn't really understand why but I did know I was excited about having an older sister. I always wanted one especially because I was the only girl in my family. In the first visit, we played games and talked about many things. I felt odd because I was so used to my big brothers at home. At home I felt secured and loved. My brothers would beat me up and care for me all at the same time. While hanging with my birth brother and sister I didn't feel the same type of love and security. It could have been because I really didn't know them that well. I left the visit still feeling confused, but I guess it was going to take a lot of time and effort from all of us.

After a couple of months my birth mother would plan visits, but never follow through with them. A few days later she would call with some excuse as to why she didn't show up. This went on for months and then she just stopped calling. I thought to myself, 'what kind of person would give their child away and when given a chance to reconnect still not take advantage? It would have been better if I had never met her. I felt worse now. At first I was angry, and then hopeful, now it just sucked. I didn't understand what was going on and it was too hard to even talk about. I didn't understand why I was hurting since I didn't want her in my life to begin with. Even still, I wondered if I said something wrong during our last visit or because I wouldn't call her mom. I mean I just didn't know. This feeling lasted for years. Just when I thought I got over it, she popped up again. Just like her, she showed up with more excuses.

Hey! Meek, you know I want to apologize for not showing up all those times. It won't happen again. I just got a little busy you know, trying to get things right for us.

She was taking me through the motions all over again, but what was I supposed to do? Like any child, I accepted her back in. I thought it would be different this time. My biological sister was a little older than me so she tried to step up and visited with me on her own time. I was excited about hanging out with my big sister. I felt great when I hung around her. I even wanted to be like her when I grew up. We had started to form a really good relationship until one day she showed me another side of her. She was very bitter and upset a lot. She said things to me that made me lose all respect for her. She would often talk to me about my family. She would always tell me that they weren't my real family. It always made me feel upset and angry with her. Those types of conversations went on for a while and made my life that much more complicated to deal with. I would hear her saying those things to me even when I tried to fall asleep. She would also tell me that my family really couldn't love me. I didn't know what to do about the conversations. I started getting even more confused as to who loved me and who my family was. I even began to behave differently around my family. The things she was saying to me began to get into my head. I guess my sister was just as confused and hurt as I was. They say that hurt people hurt people. One minute she would tell me, 'that's not your real family', and the next minute she was upset at our birth mother for leaving us all behind. I held my head down and thought that maybe being like my sister was not the best thing to do anymore. I needed someone to rescue me from these hurtful feelings that seemed to thicken by the moment. My visits with my biological sister faded and it was back to the drawing board.

It seemed as if my inner battles eventually found their way into my school and social life. I was a very out-going, friendly, and loving individual who always found laughter to be a wonderful thing. I guess I had to make myself laugh to keep from crying. I was getting older and for some reason the hurt was getting stronger. It was a long while before I had heard anything from my birth family and by this time I was getting ready to enter into high school. I made it to the last week of school without getting into trouble all year.

The bell rang and classes were in session. The teacher was calling the roll. "Shameka Staley", called the teacher. Just like always, I responded, "I am here". Out of nowhere, one of my classmates screamed, "hey! Staley tell me something. Why is your last name different from your brothers? What is that all about?" I tried to play it off and just responded with a nonchalant, "nothing". To my displeasure, he didn't let it die down. "What do you mean nothing", he said. Finally the teacher called the class to attention and began her lesson for the day.

I felt like my life was a roller coaster that was never coming to an end. Reflecting back, I realized that my life was pretty strange. My birth mom misspelled my name at birth and gave me her last name. However the family that raised me had a different last name than mine. I never really talked about it to my friends, so I guess that seemed a little odd. My friends tried to ask me about my name, but I just avoided it as much as possible. This particular day I didn't handle it so well, especially with everything going on with my birth family and all. After school, my brother came to meet me in front of my class. Normally he would wait for me outside, but not this particular day. I knew someone must have told him what happened in class. My brother Anthony was about three years older than I was, but we were very close. He didn't play any games when it came to me. Even when I was a little baby he would watch over me day and night. As soon as he saw me, Anthony said, "What's wrong with you?" He had noticed that my behavior toward the family was a bit distant. I didn't want to tell him what was wrong because I knew he would get upset with my birth family and I didn't want that to happen. Although I was really hurting and upset, I still loved them and didn't want any problems between the two families. Finally I broke down and told him how my sister said all those things about my family and it made me feel really bad. Anthony actually took it better than I expected. He told me that no matter what anybody said, I will always be a part of the family. He also mentioned that he loved me and I would always be his little sister. I explained to him that I wasn't sure if I ever wanted to visit with my birth sister again mainly because I didn't like the negative things she would say to me. He told me that everything would be alright and I didn't have to visit with those people if I didn't want to. I held that conversation dear to me and it made me feel safe. I believed my brother and trusted his words, but deep down inside I still felt the hurt inside.

    For a long-time and maybe even still, I battled with abandonment issues. As hard as I tried to think otherwise, there were parts of me that had feelings of hate, hurt, disappointment, and the lack of being loved. Even with all of these emotions of pain, I still had hoped to connect with my birth mother. Maybe it's an innate thing to want to connect with your mom. The thought of how hard it was to tell my birth mother I loved her or even to call her mother started to cross my mind. I even thought about how difficult it has been to face my friends and classmates without feeling ashamed. It was never my intention to hurt my family by being distant, but I think I was hurting them by my actions. I seemed so unhappy and ashamed of my situation and I'm sure it tore them apart. My pillow laid tear stained night after night. Through all of this, I began to blame God for my situation and I vowed not to go to Him. I often cried myself to sleep, but that was when I could dream of falling into a shadow of open arms welcoming me back onto the deserted shore of righteousness.

Step 5: Finding A Way To Let God Back In

It seemed like I kneeled down to pray by routine, and deep down inside, I felt God was responsible for my situation. I mean, how could this happen to me? I never ask to be here and on top of that my own birth mother gave me up. Believing that this was all a part of my purpose or that God knew what He was doing was way beyond my scope of thinking. It was amazing because even with all my anger and doubt, I heard God inviting me back to Him. It was at that moment that I decided to accept His invitation.

Dear God, forgive me for being so selfish and unwilling to obey, but I am hurting. The thought of knowing I have a birth mother who seems unsure about wanting to be a part of my life and a birth father who knows nothing about me being his daughter affects me tremendously. I know things haven't been easy between me and you, but I don't know who else to blame for a situation like this. Since I found out about my situation, things have been very hard for me. I was better off not knowing. I find myself not being able to sleep good at night, daydreaming during the day, separating myself from everyone else, and feeling empty. I wonder if this is my fault, whether this is the result of my sins. I search my life, but I can't find anything in me that would deserve such a consequence Lord. I don't like feeling this way inside. I don't like separating myself from everyone, especially my loving family who has been there for me since the beginning. Lord, I say all this to say, I'm sorry. As I rest on my knees, I beg you to come back into my life. I am also asking for another chance to open up again toward my family and friends. Give me a chance to tell my friends about my situation without feeling ashamed. God, I know that forgiveness toward my birth family is the right thing to do, but how? How do I look pasted my hurt? Forgiving my birth mother may be right, but it feels so wrong on the inside. I hurt so deeply Lord. Lord, help me to be delivered from this. Help me to forgive. God, as I get up from here, help me to take my first step toward the life you want for me.

Once I got up, I knew that I had to tell people close to me about my situation. I wrestled with it for a while because it shouldn't matter if they knew or not, but I realized that telling them wasn't for them, but for me. I needed to relieve myself of the shame that I wore like a coat. I didn't know who to tell first, but my best friend Nicole seemed like the best choice. I decided to tell her after our next basketball practice.

I was anxious and before I knew it, the bell sounded to end the school day, which signaled that I had a few minutes to get to basketball practice. Practice was intense as always, but once again we made it through. Shortly after practice Nicole and I were walking out of the locker room and that's when I decided to tell her. Of course I fumbled over my words while I was trying to start up the conversation.

"Hey Nicole, sit down for a minute I have something to share with you." I was so nervous, but I continued on. "Do you remember how you always ask me why my last name is different from my brothers' last name?"

She had a blank stare, wondering where I was coming from, but responded, "Yes I remember".

"Well when I was about a week old, my birth mother decided that taking care of me was something she was unable to do, so she ask my mother and father if they could keep me until she got things together. Well as you can see things are still not together."

She was almost speechless. "WOW! Are you serious", she screamed.
"Yes I am."

"Do you think she is coming back for you? "

"I don't think so. I mean she visits from time to time, but my mother told me it would be up to me if I wanted to go back, but I can't see myself with any other family. I mean don't get me wrong; sometimes I wonder what things would be like, but not enough to leave my family."

"Did your birth mother have any other children?" It seemed like Nicole had a bunch of questions, but it finally felt good to talk to someone about things.

"Yes I have an older sister and brother. My oldest sister lives with her father's mother and my brother lives with my birth mother's mother."

"You mean to tell me your birth mother gave them up too?"

"Yep. She kept them for a while on and off, but that's about all."

"I can't believe that someone could do such I thing."

"Yes well I guess that makes two of us. I always thought that if you had children then you were supposed to raise them. I guess I was wrong."

"I mean Meek so how does something like that make you feel?"

"For real Nicole I have been trying to deal with it since my mother told me and it has not been easy. I spend most of my time blaming God and other people because I don't know what else to do. It hurts so much and a lot of times I find myself doing more crying than anything else. I distance myself from my family, but cannot seem to understand why."

"WOW! That's a lot to swallow all at one time. It seems like you have been holding it in for some time."

"Yes you can say that again, but it feels good to finally tell you. Thank you for listening."

"So you say you visit with your birth family sometimes?"

"Yes I had a few visits here and there, but it was kind of weird most of the time."

"What do you mean weird", Nicole asked.

"Just think about it Nicole. My mom is the only mom I know. She's raised me since I was a week old."

"Ok but why is that weird", she asked again.

"It's weird because when I am with my birth mother I don't even know what to call her." "What! So how do you start up a conversation with her?"

"Easy. I just walk up to her and start talking. I know it sounds crazy, but that's how it is I guess. I never tell her I love her when she says it to me."

"How about your sister and brother? Do you get along with them", she questioned.

"Well you know I always wanted a big sister and having another big brother isn't so bad either."

"Ok and I am waiting for you to tell me what it's like hanging out with them."

"Well I didn't get much time to hang out with my brother you know how guys are. They like to do their own thing. I was excited about having a big sister, but after a while the excitement faded away."

"Why do you say that? You always wanted a sister, how could the excitement fade away?"

"I mean when we first started visiting with each other, it was real cool. I would look forward to hanging out with her. It was great, but after a while she turned out not to be what I wanted. She spent most of her time trying to tell me my family wasn't my birth family as if I already didn't know. It got really difficult to hang around her so when the visits slowed down I wasn't mad at all."

"Man Meek. This is all so crazy. So how are you after hearing and living all of this?"

"I actually felt worst now that I have spent time with her. I try to take into consideration that she feels some kind of way toward my birth mother and that was her way of taking out her frustration. Even though I know otherwise, what she says still rings in my ears and makes me question things."

"Well Meek it seems like you are probably not the only one affected. Look at it this way, if your birth mother would have never gave you up we would not be friends today."

"Yes I guess you are right in more ways than one, but can we please talk about something else? I am starting to get a little emotional."

The conversation with Nicole was heavy, but it was necessary. She was always good at trying to make a joke so she did just that and we laughed it off. The joke was our way of moving away from that subject and talking about something else. After all that talking our rides were here and it was time to go home. We said our goodbyes and went on with the rest of our day. While riding home I started day dreaming once again. I must admit it felt kind of good to talk about my situation with someone, but I often wondered if I could tell my story to others without being judged or looked at funny. Nicole was my friend so I didn't feel like she would judge me, but I knew she has a bunch of thoughts going through her head as she rode home. Maybe I was looking too far into things instead of letting things take their natural course. My prayer was for help in taking the first step into opening up and He heard my prayers. He did His part and I would do mine. I decided to not hold things in anymore. I am proud of myself. I finally told someone. That was alright, it didn't hurt one bit. Looking up into the skies on the ride home I found myself entering into yet another conversation with God.

Well God as you can see I am back again. I know you are happy to hear from me two times within the same week. I know you thought it would take me a minute. Truth is so did I? Today I accomplished a big step and that was telling someone about my situation. Who knows maybe tomorrow I could tell someone else. Yea right, He and I both knew that I was joking, but humor is good.

My brother looked into the rear view mirror and asked if I was crazy. "Well what are you laughing at," he snickered. Shaking my head, I responded, "nothing big bro, just an inside joke". "Inside joke you say. Let's see if you think this is funny", he laughed. Blasting country music was his idea of torture. He did that often, especially in the mornings when he took me to school. He would turn the radio up as high as it could go and drive slowly in front of all my friends. I guess that's his way of embarrassing me and it works because my friends find it so funny. We finally arrived at home and I jumped out of the car and ran into the house. I was ready to get out of those smelly basketball clothes and into a nice hot shower. When I walked through the door, my wonderful mother was standing there with a smile on her face ready to great me with open arms. Like always, after a shower and getting settled, I began my homework. My mother didn't play. We were on a routine and it never skipped a beat.

While in the shower I found myself drifting back into the conversation I was having earlier with God. This time I expressed how I was ready for a new outlook on things. I wanted to continue taking steps forward instead of backwards. It was time I stopped pointing fingers and allowing my situation to hold me be back. I understood that it would take some time, but I was willing to give it a try. I felt really good. I don't know why. Maybe it had a lot to do with me getting ready to start high school. Anyway God let me end this conversation because I am starting to ramble and my feet are getting wrinkled from being in this shower too long. I would like to close out by saying thank you for giving me another chance and allowing me to take it a step forward.

Step 6: A New Outlook On Life

Well it was time for high school and I was ready for my new outlook on life. I was willing to put the past behind me and was determined to think positive. From time to time I thought about what life would be like if conversations with my birth family would have continued, but I was moving on. The New Year was in session and time was starting to fly by very quickly. I was getting a feel of what being in high was all about and I must admit it wasn't so bad. Of course being a freshman you always had the older students to pick on you every once in a while, but it didn't last long. It wasn't too bad for me anyway because all of my friends from middle school were there along with one of my older brothers Anthony. Anthony was supposed to be the ladies' man; every time you look around he was messing with somebody's girlfriend. He spent more time out of class than in class. It was always, 'your brother is doing this or he just did that. It was crazy, but always funny. Although my brother never really went to class and stayed in troubled, it was always quiet as kept when we got home.

I was excited about the new look in my life at the time. I was hanging out with my friends more and playing basketball with the big girls. Playing ball in high school was a lot different than middle school. In high school it was about working hard to get a position and keeping it. I was on the move and it was no time for me to think twice about anything else going on at the moment.

Moving swiftly through ninth and tenth grade with still no contact from my birth family, I continued to keep myself extra busy. After a while I started preparing myself for the next step, which happened to be college preparation. Most of my friends had everything all planned out. They knew what needed to be done for college because someone in their family was in college or had attended college. As for me I would be the first one in my family to attend college. I didn't have a clue about what I was doing, so when my friends decided to have those long boring conversations about college, my mouth was shut.

"Hello girls, what's going on", I said to my friends. Nothing much, just sitting here trying to get this paper work completed for college was Nicole's reply. When she began to ask me about my college paperwork, I was so overwhelmed at all they had already completed and how far behind I really was. I was so happy when the bell rang and marked the time to go home. I left quickly before they could ask me anything else about college.

On my way home I started thinking about why I wanted to go to college. I knew it was expected, but I had no real reason. Maybe it would make my parents proud or maybe going to college would help me take care of them someday. After all, I do owe them that much. They didn't have to take me in. I also figured that I should go to college because all my friends were going. It also entered my mind that I wanted to go to college to do something for myself, to complete something. Even though I didn't know why I wanted to go to college, I knew that I wanted to work with kids, particularly young teenage girls faced with abuse or neglect. I think I would be a good person for them to relate to. Who knows, maybe one day I could start a business of my own that would provide services for the youth. When I got home I didn't say much to anyone. After all it was a very long and stressful day. I spent the majority of my time racking my brain about going to college. My mother noticed that faraway look on my face and she asked me about it. I tried to tell her it was nothing, but she wasn't going for that

"Don't give me that. Tell me what's wrong", she said. I found it really difficult to lie to my mom or at least to be good at lying to my mom, so I just started to tell her what I felt. "Well Mom, I was thinking about going to college, but..." Before I could even finish my sentence, she interrupted, "but what... listen I don't want you to think going to college will make us any more proud of you than we already are. If you decide to go, make sure it is something you want to do for yourself. Trust and believe if you decide to go, we will support your dream all the way." My mom is always so reassuring to me. "I know, but ma, I don't know if I have what it takes to make it in college." That was the truth. I think my fear came from just being unsure about whether I could do it. "I believe you will do just fine", she reassured me again, "we are so proud of you and whatever you do in life; I know you will be successful at it. Momma raised you well baby so don't be afraid. You will be alright."

I actually felt a little better. That's a mother's touch I guess. She may not be my biological mother, but she's never made me feel like I didn't belong to her. Well after talking to my mother, I decided to follow my heart.

With my newfound assurance, I was excited about getting to school. School was always fun and important to me, but this time I had some important business to handle. After arriving to school, I went directly to the guidance counselor's office to set an appointment about college preparation. After meeting with my counselor, I knew exactly what had to be done. I was a little nervous about taking the SAT since test taking was always my weak area, so I decided to keep putting it off. My friends and family would ask me about college, but I never would say much about it. Just like everything else in my life, I decided to run away from it. It's funny how I was really excited about college at one point only to be deterred by the idea of having to take a test.

11th grade finally came to an end and it was time to enjoy the summer. I was hanging out with my family and friends, attending church, and playing basketball all summer long. In order to run from the things going on in my life, I stayed busy. I wish they had all-night activities as well that way I would be set straight. Nighttime was the hardest time for me because that's when I thought about what I was running from. I even struggled with finding a way for the hurt in my heart to disappear but there was no remedy. From the outside looking in, it was if I had it going on, no worries, happy-go-lucky, down to earth girl who loved to have fun. If I could turn myself inside out, I would actually shock a lot of people. I tried to escape from the hurt, but it would never go away. I don't know maybe one day soon I will be able to start overcoming my challenges, but until then I had to do what I did best, run for the border.

Well we all know how time flies when you're having fun. I had made it through another summer, but now it was time to face my last year in high school. I was in my senior year and still had not taken the SAT test. I contemplated that test for weeks and finally decided to take a shot at it. I went to my guidance counselor and signed up for the SAT test. This test would determine if I get into college so I was very nervous about it. Anyway I completed the test and managed to accomplish at least one of my challenges. I actually felt good on the inside and outside. WOW! That was something special. Well after taking the test I started to complete and send out college applications. Then a new nervousness came upon me. I was nervous about getting accepted into college and the thought not passing my test played over and over in my head. The time was passing and all of my friends already knew the college they were attending. Unlike me, they actually started preparing during our junior year. Trying to wait patiently for responses I continued to go through my senior year of school with an outside smile. Every day after school I would check the mail waiting for a response from the colleges I applied to. The letters started coming back but it wasn't looking good for me. Waiting patiently was quickly turning into desperation.

Basketball season was just about over and so was the school year, but still no signs of a college acceptance. Even when I was anxious about the whole situation, my family stepped in big time and just encouraged me to hold on and be patient. My brother Anthony always told me not to worry about it that everything was going to work itself out. I knew he believed in me, but truthfully I wasn't sure if I believed in myself.

With two months left in the school year, one day I rushed home to check the mail only to find no mail in the box. As I walked in the house, my mother calls me into the room and hands me an envelope from Johnson C. Smith University, one of my last applications completed. Standing in the room waiting was none other than my three brothers, and father. As I open the letter and started reading tears rolled down my face. Unsure about the tears being happy or sad, my family waited patiently for a response. Holding my head up while wiping the tears from my face I announced congratulations I have been accepted.

Say what are you serious my mother said, yes I am. Let me see my brother Anthony said, Wow! It's true you actually got accepted. Man my little sister is going away to college.

Man I immediately started thanking God. Almost instantly, my mother along with the rest of my family hugged me tight saying congratulations and we knew you could do it. My family was so happy to spread the word that their baby girl would be the first in the generation to complete college. After everyone cleared the room, I decided to take a minute or two for God to tell Him thank You. Even when I didn't believe in myself, He believed in me.

I guess this new outlook isn't so bad after all. God I know I have a long way to go with trusting and opening up, but please hang in there with me.

It was time for me to get ready for the next day of school. After all I had so many people to tell the good news. The next day in school I was happy to announce my acceptance into college. Celebrating together my friends and I went out for dinner. We talked about how we'd all stay in touch and how we thought life would be in college. My best friend Nicole and I were actually going to both be in North Carolina, while all the others would be spread out in different states.

"I am so excited..." said Nicole, "we are all going away to college. I mean just yesterday it seem like we were starting high school." I jumped in and said, "I know right, this is going to be something to remember." "So guys we need to plan our first visit with each other", said Nicole. I thought it would only be right if the first group visit be in North Carolina since both Nicole and I were in North Carolina. It would be the smartest idea to me. Everyone agreed so it was settled.

We all finished up our dinner, hugged one another and left as if it was going to be our last time with one another until the first break in college.

High school was finally over and summer was taking its course. We hung out a little bit, but not as much as we did while in school. We were all trying to work small jobs so we could make money to take with us while in college. All work and hardly any room for play made the summer go by very fast and it was now time to off to college.

I was scheduled to visit Johnson C. Smith for a tour and they needed other important information. The school was in Charlotte, North Carolina, which happens to be about two and half hours away from my home. After the weekend stay in Charlotte, my parents were excited, nervous, and somewhat concerned about the tuition and how they would be able to afford sending me there. Without receiving any scholarships and being eligible for limited financial aid, the tuition and fees seemed like it would be rather expensive. My father always wanted his little girl to be happy so he decided to take out a loan large enough to cover all the extra expenses. His justification was that he was so proud of me. My mother wasn't really sure my dad should take the loans out.

"Babe are you sure this is something you want to do", my mother said, "I mean taking out this loan is a big commitment." My dad simply replied, "I know baby, but I want our daughter to know how much going to college means to us. Think about it she would be the first one in our family to attend college and possibly finish college. We have made so many sacrifices for our children and I believe God will bless us for that."

I was sitting so patiently in the back of the car as they drove back home from the college, trying not to listen to the conversation, but I couldn't help to overhear the conversation between my parents. I thought about waiting or trying to get into a college at home, but then I thought about all of the plans my friends and I made just before we got out of high school. I mean what would they think if I wasn't able to attend school at this time because of money? This would mess up our plans all together. I couldn't let that happen. After all I've been through, I deserved a break. At least that's what I thought. My parents did not question their decision. They stuck with their initial agreement to take out a loan so that I could go to Johnson C. Smith.

At first I struggled with being away from home along with getting used to the college life. After a while things started to pick up, I started meeting new people to hang out with and different activities to get involved in.

Things were actually going pretty good I was finally started to sleep at night without tossing and turning. I remember waking up smiling because I had such a wonderful night sleep, but just when I thought it was ok to smile my phone started ringing. I had to answer it because my roommate was not in the room. I answered the phone and it was none other than my birth mother. I was thinking to myself, "why now after all these years". I continued on with the conversation just waiting for the excuses to start up.

"Hey! Meek, how are you? I know it's been a minute, but I have been trying to get myself together. You know, so we can all be a family. I got me a new friend and he is a lot different than the others. He actually wants to meet you one day. I hope that's ok with you. I am so proud of all my kids. Your sister and brother are already in college and now my baby girl is just getting started in college. I am so blessed to have such smart kids. I want to come and see you next weekend so that I can take you out and buy you some clothes for school. Would you like that?" I was so floored that my only response was, "yea, I guess that will be okay".

We got off the phone and I was actually mad at myself because I didn't have the guts to tell her what was really on my mind, as usual I held it in. Even though I didn't tell her how I really felt, I was happy to hear from her. Just as I expected, she didn't show up. It was even more upsetting because she is clueless how each disappointment breaks me down. It is almost as if she spends her spare time creating ways to hurt me. Even after years of countless lies, I still looked out for her call or waited for an impromptu visit. Needless to say, I was often disappointed. I found myself falling into a deep depression and my grades took the brunt of it. Not only were my grades poor, I started to spend less time studying and practicing basketball and more time hanging out with friends.

The school year had come to an end. I didn't do as well as I should have, but that seemed to be the least of my troubles. Soon after the semester ended, I received a letter telling me I had exceeded my funds and needed to take another loan out for the upcoming year. I didn't want to be such a hardship on my parents, but my father was willing to take out another loan even though he and my mom couldn't afford the initial loan. Maybe he felt compelled to make a way since he walked out on us years ago. I guess in his mind he felt like he owed it to me. He didn't come back home until my senior year. By this time my brothers were no longer boys, they were men living in their own homes and getting ready to raise their own families. My dad often felt like he had to make up for lost time.

My mother was against taking out another large loan just so I could go to a school far from home. She suggested that I consider a school closer to home and possibly getting a job. She tried to explain her reasoning to my dad that she raised us to be independent, strong, and determined, but she emphasized that she taught us to be thoughtful and responsible. She didn't find it very thoughtful or responsible to put the family in a financial bind when there were more cost efficient alternatives. She explained to him that it would be selfish to stretch the family financially in order for me to remain at my school. My dad understood, but he explained to her that he wanted his children to have the best and that in some ways he felt compelled to repay the family so to speak. This is the reason that I love my mother so much. Her response was, "I don't want you to feel like you owe us for lost times. Let the past be the past and pick up from here as if you never left." Only my mom forgives wholeheartedly. She explained that she already forgave him, but he needed to forgive himself. She also let him know that this is a part of growing up for me and accepting responsibility for my success and future. She wouldn't allow me to make a selfish decision and cause such a financial burden for our family.

The lesson sounded great and my mother posed it to me, but I didn't want to hear any parts of me not returning to school. I was engulfed in what others would think if I had to change schools for financial reasons. I avoided the subject and hoped my dad would just take out the loan. I was not thinking of the family, but rather what everyone would think of me. My mother was so disappointed in me for my indecision and selfishness and she had no problems letting me know.

"Do you realize how selfish and inconsiderate you are? Your father took out a loan for you to attend college although we didn't have the money from the beginning. We drove up and down the highway to pick you up, buy you groceries, pay extra money for books, and borrowed money, all so you could have what you needed this year," she screamed. "Even your brothers contributed. They didn't want you to work while in school so they sent money to us for you and you mean to tell me that this is how you respond. You haven't yet to say thank you or show some form of appreciation. I get it, you feel entitled", she finished. Even after the stern tongue lashing, all I could do was cry and blame everyone else. I tried to blame everything on the circumstances. I really had a 'woe is me' attitude.

I didn't think so at the time, but luckily for me, my mother didn't want to hear my pitiful response. She let me know that I needed to look at myself instead of everyone else. To top it off, she also told me that I had to start looking for a job immediately. My mother got up and told me to stop pointing fingers unless I was pointing at myself. You would think that I would have learned my lesson, but when she left my room, I convinced myself that she didn't understand and if she lived the life that I did, she'd think differently. I thought maybe it was because of my situation or it due to the fact that my father had abandoned us for so many years, but truth be told, it was me. My only concern was how my friends perceived me. I didn't care about the debt I was putting my family in. I really needed to do something about this character flaw, but I wasn't so sure about where to start.

Step 7: Finding My Biological Father

Taking a step towards ownership, I decided to make up for my selfishness. I immediately started applying for jobs and to the local universities. By the end of the week I had a job at a fast food restaurant. Two weeks after starting my job, I received a letter of acceptance for the fall semester at Claflin University located in Orangeburg, South Carolina, my hometown. Things were looking up. I guess my mother was right about the positives of taking responsibility for my own future.

It seems as if the summer zoomed by, mainly because I was busy working. I was even able to add a second part-time job as a receptionist at my sister-in-law's hair salon. My sister-in-law was a very positive role model in my life. She started dating my brother, Anthony toward the end of my junior year in high school. She immediately became a positive impact in my life. It was almost like filling the gap of the sister I always wanted. She was the type that didn't say much, but could feel you out just by being around you. She was the only woman that didn't take any stuff from my brother. She always made me feel comfortable and I never hesitated to talk to her if something was on my mind. I was so thankful that she and my brother let me work at the hair salon. It was my responsibility to clean up the shop and, she and I would be the last ones to leave the shop. During those times, we would catch up on small talk. Madeca always showed concern and encouragement towards me. She called me Temerk, which is actually the name given to me at birth. I've always hated that name, but she loved it for some odd reason. Somehow hearing it from her did not make it sound as bad. She actually still calls me Temerk until this day. Spending so much time with Madeca allowed her to notice anytime my mood changed and she was able to pick right up on it. One Friday after working the full day, she noticed something different and immediately asked me about it. Of course I really didn't want to talk about it. She didn't pry, but she had a way of getting me to talk without me even knowing it.

"Temerk, I know something is wrong. Tell me what it is," Madeca said. "Well it's nothing really sister; for some reason I have really been doing a lot of thinking about my biological father. I am not sure why, but it seems like the older I get, the more I wonder what he's like", I responded. It was something I've never said to anyone and she was surprised to even hear me voice that I thought about him. I tried to tell her that it's something that's always on my mind, but I try to keep it away from the forefront and let the past remain in the past. That's easier said than done though. I also try to understand why this happened. I try to open up, I try to forget about wanting to know what my birth family is really like, but I can't forget. I can't forgive and I can't seem to open my heart. She was floored by my admission. "Temerk, I can't say I know exactly what you are going through or how you feel, but think about it like this, everything happens for a reason. God blessed you with a wonderful family who loves and cares a great deal about you. God knew what he was doing before you even came into this world and placing you with this family was part of the plan. No one said it would ever be easy, but just hang in there. Stay encouraged and take one day at a time. When the time is right, you will meet your biological father and find peace within for your birth family," advised Madeca. Her words always calmed me down and put things in a greater perspective.

I finished cleaning the shop and went home so I could get ready for my first day of school. It was a little hard for me to get excited because I never wanted to attend college at home. I always thought attending college at home wasn't the cool thing to do, but I had to suck it up. I knew I had to make the best of it, so that's what I did.

Halfway through the fall semester, I started to get a little excited about the choices I was making in my life thus far even while attending a local college. I decided to pledge in a sorority, but in order for me to do that I had to make sure my grades were up to standard before the year was over. I was on my grind attending classes during the morning time and work during the evening. Managing two jobs and being a full-time student was a bit much, but I was working it out. As I started to get older, I realized one great quality about myself and that was if I put my mind to it, there was no stopping me.

The following year I started meeting new friends and decided to pledge that year as well. I decided to pledge Zeta Phi Beta Sorority Inc. during the fall semester of 2001. During that time, I took on responsibilities as both Chaplin and phylactery. I was very dedicated to the organization, receiving awards for the most dedicated soror, and soror of the year.

I was actually starting to find things that made me happy I was attending church as always, but now I would invite friends to come along with me. Things were happening at a fast past in my life at the time and I was trying my best to keep up. After a about another month or so I decided to take a leave of absence at my part-time job at the fast food restaurant. I was still working at the shop, but of course I had to let something go for a minute so I could stay on track.

This particular day was no different than most. I was on my way to work after class but this specific day I started to feel a little sick so I decided to call my sister-in-law to let her know I was not feeling well. It seemed noisy and busy when I called so I just pressed my way in to be of some help at the shop. Just like normal, I came in and made sure the stylists and my sister-in-law were okay. Noticing that everything seemed in order, I proceeded to the front desk and began working on my homework. After almost thirty minutes, I faintly heard someone calling my voice. Going to the back to see if I heard correctly, I found Madeca in the back with a young lady. I didn't think anything of her presence since often times people that I didn't know frequented the shop.

"Hey sister, what can I do for you today," I responded as I entered the back office. She explained to me that the visitor was actually my cousin. My immediate thought was 'who cares', but I just stood there waiting for a further explanation. The awkward silence gave the young lady an opportunity to talk. She said, "I am your first cousin. Your birth father and my father are brothers. My eyes lit up although unsure of what to say or think next, I vaguely remember hearing that I had an uncle that lived nearby. I thought little of it since I believed that my father knew nothing of my existence. My newfound cousin immediately called her father and then asked me the question I secretly been yearning to hear. "Would you like to meet your father?" I stood there dumbfounded for about ten seconds. I didn't even understand how her father knew about me. Madeca had actually talked to her client about me and in their conversation they concluded that I possibly had an uncle living nearby by the name of B. Bowman. It turned out that B. Bowman was actually her father. The young lady started telling me about my father and how he would be so happy to see me. I always assumed that my father didn't know about me, but my cousin advised me that my father and my family found out about me years ago. She told me that my biological brother would remind them every chance that he got. She also let me know that the family's annual reunion was coming up and that I should go. All of this was overwhelming. I just stood there. My cousin gave me her number and told me to call her if I decided to go. I couldn't think of anything else to say so I just asked Madeca if I could go home for the rest of the day.

My mother knew something was odd as soon as she saw me. I had a puzzled look on my face. I sat there for a few minutes trying to find a way to explain what just happened at the hair salon. I plainly told her that my birth father knew about me, but still made no attempt to contact me. My mother consoled me, but told me not to get beside myself until I knew the whole story. "So tell me how did this all come about, how did you learn about your father," my mother asked. I could only respond that oddly enough a client was actually my first cousin. I told my mom that the girl's dad lives nearby in Orangeburg and his name is B. Bowman. I also told my mother that their family reunion was approaching and my newfound cousin had invited me. She was apprehensive since it was so soon, but she thought it was a great idea for me to meet my paternal family. I was excited, but still a little nervous. This is something that I always wanted, but never actually thought it would happen. My mom and I both agreed that I should give it some thought. She never told me otherwise, but I know she had some reservations about me meeting with people that even she had never met. One of the things I loved so much about my mother, is she never shared her apprehensions, but encouraged me to think and pray on it and make my own decision.

A few days went by and I was still shocked about the situation. I spent most of my time trying to decide if I was going to the reunion, thinking what it would be like if I did. Finally after days of contemplating I decided to call my cousin and accept the invitation. She was so excited that I was going to go. She told me that she would pick me up on Saturday and to make sure that I was ready on time. We had some more small talk, but she ended the conversation making sure that I was clear on everything and had no further questions. I told her that I would call her back if I could think of anything else.

The rest of the week was a whirlwind. Saturday came in no time at all. I was nervous, excited, scared, and confused all at the same time. I began to get so overwhelmed thinking I have never traveled this far away from home, much less in the company of people I barely knew. I tried not to overthink, but that didn't work. I found myself falling right back to that train of thought. Good thing that my crazy thoughts didn't stop Saturday from coming. That morning I got up finished packing, ate breakfast and was ready to go. I was so nervous and scared that I almost started crying. I knew if my mom and dad saw me crying that they would not have wanted me to go. I couldn't let that happen. I've been waiting for this moment for thirteen years since I learned of my adoption. While I was sitting in the living room, my brother Anthony came in and gave me a big hug. He said, "Don't worry sis, everything is going to be alright. We are only a phone call away". That calmed me down. Soon enough my ride arrived and it was time for me to leave. My family walked me outside with a look that wondered if I was going to return. My parents tried their best to hold in the tears, as they both walked me toward the van.

As we prepared ourselves to pull off, my father told my uncle to take care of me and to call once we made it. My mother closed the door to the van and stepped back. We pulled off, as we drove away I looked back and noticed my mother, father, brothers and sister-in-law standing there waving goodbye.

I wanted to tell my uncle to stop the van and let me out, but I knew this was something I had to do. I gazed out of the window until I could no longer see my house or my family.

"Hey Meek, do you know anything about your father", asked my cousin. I answered honestly and told her that I really didn't know anything about him. From my understanding, my birth mother never told my father that I was his child. While listening to everything and processing during the car ride, I guess for all these years my father thought he only had a son by my birth mother. To quell those thoughts, my uncle jumped into the conversation only to say that my father knew about me for some time now. "Well you know we found out from both your birth brother and mother. "Your mother finally told us about you," he countered. "What do you mean he knows about me?" The questions flew out of my mouth. My uncle simply told me that he didn't know much, but that approximately ten years after I was born, the family was told that there was a possibility that I was J. Bowman's daughter. Your birth brother, whom the family knows very well, reminds us of you all the time. The obvious question, which swarmed my brain, finally came out. "Why didn't anyone say anything to me?" They're response was that my father was unsure since my mother always assured him that I wasn't his child. Trying to slightly change the mood, my cousin began to tell me of all my siblings that I would meet at the reunion. It turns out that through my father, I have one older brother, one older sister, and a younger brother and sister. Along with my other birth brother from my mother, there were six of us. In addition to that, I also have two step sisters since my father had recently got married. I asked if my father knew about me coming to the reunion. "Yes," my uncle said, "I spoke with him about it a few days ago and he seemed to be very excited about you coming." That reply made me feel a little bit better. My uncle let me know that it was a thirteen-hour drive and that we had one more stop to pick up my grandmother. Thirteen hours was plenty of time to mull over all of this new information.

I tried to picture what it was going to be like meeting my birth father and siblings, especially my younger sister. After all this time I am finally going to be someone's big sister. I started smiling to myself. I was both anxious and nervous about this day in which I had dreamed about.

I waited patiently in the car while we stopped to pick up my grandmother. I wondered if I would look like her. She politely got in and spoke and asked how I was doing. I don't know what I expected, but I hoped for a more warm response. For goodness sake, I was her grandchild that she had never met. She spoke to me as a mere courtesy. After that moment, I started to wonder if I was going to get the same treatment from my birth father and siblings. I was beginning to think that this was a bad idea. Feeling a little ashamed confused, and somewhat disappointed, I finally managed to doze off into somewhat of a deep sleep.

I woke up just in time. After several hours of riding we finally reached our destination. I immediately gathered my things and proceeded to take them out of the van. While taking my belongings out of the van I could hear my uncle and grandmother having a conversation about me.

"Hey Ma. Do you know if John told his other children about Meek," my uncle asked. "I don't think so. As a matter of fact, I don't think a lot of the family really knows about her yet. I think John is still under a little shock and doesn't really know how to break it down to everyone," she responded. "Well I hope he can figure out something because we have brought her a long way to meet him and she is looking forward to it." "I know what you mean let's just hope for the best."

It was almost like I was a secret that no one wanted to discuss. Anyway I managed to maintain my composure long enough to get upstairs and out my clothes. On the way upstairs I asked my cousin if my father was at the hotel yet. She didn't know, but said she'd call him once we got upstairs. I was in the shower at the time when my uncle came in the room to speak with his daughter. While he was talking to her, I overheard the conversation only to find out that the majority of the family knew nothing about me. My birth father was staying in a room downstairs with his wife and apparently he, his wife, my uncle, cousin, and grandmother were the only ones who knew anything about me.

"What do you mean no one really knows about her?" said Tonya. "Well, apparently it is still somewhat of a shock and has yet to be released," was his response. "Oh my gosh Dad. I feel so bad. I invited her to come all the way down here thinking that everyone knew. I don't want her to be humiliated". My uncle reassured her that everything would work out and that I was family and ultimately everyone deserved to know. "What are you saying? Are you going to tell everyone," asked my cousin. "No ma'am, I'm not. That's my brother's job, not mine," he responded.

I pushed the door open so they would know I was about to come out of the bathroom. I waited for a few seconds giving myself enough time to pull it together and them enough time to end the conversation. While I was walking out of the bathroom, the phone in the hotel room started ringing. My cousin answered the phone.

"Hello."

"Hey," a deep voice said on the other end. "How are you guys over there? I see you all made it in ok."

"Who is this?"

"This is your Uncle John. Is my daughter in the room with you?"

"Hold, on"

Here goes nothing. I picked up the phone and said hello. He asked how I was doing and engaged in other awkward small talk. "In about an hour, I would like for you to come down so we can meet," my father said. After we hung up my cousin asked me if I wanted to go for a walk. After eavesdropping on the conversation she had with her father, I had an idea of why she wanted to take a walk. As we started walking through the hotel, my cousin said, "I need to be honest with you about something".

She didn't waste any time with small talk. "When your birth father found out about you, he didn't know how to tell his children or other members of the family. He wasn't really expecting this visit from you so soon," she admitted. Hurt, disappointed, and angry, I lashed out. "Well, why did you invite me here if no one really knows anything about me?" "Well, my father and I thought it would be a good idea for you to finally meet your father and your siblings. I honestly didn't know that he hadn't told anyone about you. I'm sorry." She responded honestly and it confirmed what I overheard in the conversation with both her and her father.

It was so weird to notice how much I resembled everyone at the reunion. It was amazing, I mean after all these years I was finally given the opportunity to meet other family members that looked like me. The other individuals walking were looking at me the same way. I guess they were as shocked as I was. They were probably thinking, 'who is she?' My cousin tapped me on my shoulder and I snapped back into the conversation. I faintly heard what she was saying since I was bewildered by the whole situation. Just then, we were interrupted by my uncle ushering us back into the hotel to finally meet my father. I was nervous and excited all at the same time. When I finally approached the door, I wiped my hands off on my jeans, took a deep breath and knocked on the door.

A woman's voice screeched for me to come in. Upon entering, I found a couple sitting, as if they had been waiting for me to come down. The man stood up in shock as he walked over staring at me. He seemed amazed that I looked just like him and the rest of his children. He gave me a big hug and invited me to sit down. I can only imagine what was going through his head. This had to be a bewildering moment for him as well. After all, here he is being introduced to his twenty-one year old daughter.

His response was enough for me. "Wow! You're my baby girl. I can't believe my eyes. I don't really know what to say, but I am so sorry. I didn't know. Your mother told me…."

Just before anyone could say another word there was a knock at the door. The door opened up to two more people entering the room. When they walked in, my eyes lit up as if I had just seen a ghost. No one had to tell me that they were my siblings. The resemblance was uncanny. My birth father introduced us as we all stood there for a few minutes in shock about the resemblance.

"Meek this is your oldest sister, D, and your baby brother, J. We all embraced and shared the fact that we were happy to meet each other.

I realized that my younger sister was absent and asked my father about it. He didn't seem too bothered by it, just assured me that I would get to meet her soon enough. I still found it odd that she hadn't come up with D and J. We all talked for about another fifteen minutes before everyone left the room. As I walked out the room I headed down to the pay phone to call my family.

On the way down, I was unsure of the feeling I had inside. After all these years of waiting, I finally got the chance to meet my birth father, but it wasn't like I had imagined. I don't know. Maybe I was looking too much into the situation or maybe I felt like I was still a kept secret. When I got down stairs I picked up the phone and called home.

As soon as my mom answered the phone, the barrage of questions ensued.

"How is everything? Did you meet your birth father? What is he like? Are you ok? Did you meet anyone else? And lastly, "what took you so long to call us?"

My mother asked me so many questions all at once that it was hard for me to answer without crying. I don't know if it was hearing my mother's voice or a feeling of disappointment, but I started crying.

I told her of my great expectations coming in, but now that I had met them I kind of felt like I would have been better off not knowing them or having ever met them. I didn't know why I felt so bad about the situation. I tried to consider that he didn't know about me from birth, but none of that helped. I admitted to my mom that I was tired of feeling hurt by people that were supposed to love me and be my family. "I didn't ask to be here momma," I cried. Not knowing how to soothe me, my mom simply tried to encourage me. "I know baby, but listen, let's just take it one day at a time," she told me. Keep in mind that your birth father found out about you later on in life after he moved on, remarried, and had other children. This is something that only God and time can heal, so again just enjoy your visit while you're there and give your birth father time to come around." "I guess you are right momma. I will try my best to take it one day at a time. Well I guess I better get off this phone and head back up stairs." She reminded me that she loved me and reiterated for me to take it one day at a time.

After we got off the phone, I decided to take a little walk alone so I could pull myself back together again. I pondered on what everyone thought of me, of the whole situation. I hoped they didn't think I was out to get money. I even thought about the underlying reasons as to why my youngest sister didn't come up to meet me. It seems like my wish to find my birth father was backfiring. I only wanted to hear an explanation. After all these years, my situation never made sense. My pain only grows stronger. My questions only seem harder to answer. The older I get, the more I try to run from my situations. Everyday I'm comforted by my tears while my heart cries out for help. It was as if God felt my pain as it started to rain on my head. I didn't know if I would ever be healed from this pain.

In order to maintain some semblance of having a good time, I placed my best foot forward and made my way back to the hotel. Throughout the remainder of the weekend, I had very little interactions with my birth father and siblings. I hung around my cousin and her son the majority of the time. When people asked about me, I was either explained to be a friend of the family or just brushed over as a known secret. I didn't get to meet my youngest sister until it was time for us to leave. It didn't seem as if she was too fond of me. I tried not to let it bother me and put on a happy face and braved through the introduction and awkward embraces. The weekend ended with generic hugs between my newfound immediate family and me.

The entire way home I thought about my visit and how embarrassed I felt the entire time while I was there. The ride on the way back was nice and quiet. I was happy for that since I didn't feel up to putting on any more happy faces. We couldn't get home quick enough. If I never saw any of them again, I wouldn't be mad. Seeing them had been all too painful and I never wanted to feel that embarrassment and shame again.

Well I managed to accomplish another step in my life and it was time for me to get back to my regular life. I unpacked my bags, took a shower, and prepared for the next day of classes and work. Just before I went to bed, my mother entered the room to let me know I had a phone call. I picked up the phone not wanting to hear anything out of the ordinary. But to my surprise, it was my birth mother on the other end. I mean, could God just spare me with the emotional rollercoaster that I was on? It seems that she called to hear about my visit with my paternal family. How'd she even know I went to see them?

She told me that Ross, my brother from her, had let her know about my visit. Apparently they talked to my father before and after my visit. She apologized profusely, but reminded me that she did what she thought was best for me. She told me that she was happy that I finally had the opportunity to meet them.

It always amazed me that she would try to hold conversations with me as if she didn't walk out of my life after countless lies. "So tell me. How was it?" she gushed. "How was what?" I really didn't' want to rehash the weekend and especially not with her. She tried to pry for more answers, but got the picture with each of my dry responses. I knew her all too well; farewell was coming. "Well I am going to let you go and I will send you some money in the mail this weekend," she lied. I don't know if she thought I believed those lies, but I stopped checking for her mail years ago. She wished me well and tried to convince me that she loved me, but I just ended the conversation with an okay and hung up.

I wasn't trying to be rude, but I was tired of going through the motions over and over again. I wasn't trying to make my birth mother feel bad, but the two things I struggled with the most when it came to her was saying I love you and calling her mother. I don't know if my feelings will ever change, but as of now I can't imagine saying or feeling anything different. I was on my way to sleep when my brother, Anthony, walked in the room to give me the phone.

I couldn't imagine who was on the other end. "Hello," I said. I was surprised at the voice on the other end. It was my birth father. "Hi Meek, how are you doing," he asked. I knew who it was, but questioned it anyway. "I'm fine, who is this?" I responded. "It's John, your father. I was calling to make sure you got home okay and to apologize for not being able to spend time with you this weekend. I know things seem a little crazy for you right now, but understand that things are crazy for me as well. When you were born, your mother told me not to worry because you were not my child. I didn't give it much thought until Ross kept telling me that she was lying and you were indeed my child." It was as if he was letting years of guilt off of his shoulders. I didn't even get much of a chance to respond. "Your mother finally admitted everything to me after I prodded her for answers. I was so shocked and upset that she had lied to me for all of these years. I had never met you, but people in the neighborhood told me how much you looked like me. I was happy to meet you at the reunion, but wasn't in exactly a good place to talk. I'm sorry for that," he admitted. "I just told the rest of my children. Please understand everyone's hesitation." I tried to hold in my tears, but they streamed down my face. I tried to believe everything he said, but was having a hard time. All these years, I took everyone's explanation, never really speaking my mind to anyone. He sensed my apprehension as I ended the conversation. "Please do me a favor Meek and think about coming up this summer for a few days to visit," he chimed in before I hung up. "This time we will have a better chance to talk and get to know one another." That surprised me and made me feel good. I told him that I'd think about it and get back to him soon with an answer. I tried to drift off to sleep, but thoughts of not only the last two phone calls, but the last couple of years swarmed my mind. I decided that it was time for another heart to heart talk with God.

Well God, the last few days have truly been an experience. I don't know what I am supposed to do next. I waited all these years to meet my birth father and I finally get the chance only to discover a new level of hurt and confusion. I know everything happens for a reason, but this is a lot to take in right now. Why does it seem like my past is following me everywhere I go? Did I do something wrong? Is there anybody else out there going through what I am going through? How can I make it if my past keeps following me? I know I said one day at a time, but is it possible to skip to the future without my past? Some are saying take it one day at a time, others are saying forget it. I sometimes want to ask them if faced with the same situation, what their reaction would be. Instead God, I turn to you.

"What does one say?"

Life is full of
Trials
Disappointment
Understatement
Disbelief
Hurt

We cry
We laugh
We hide
Behind our inner feelings
Only making things worse

We face situations everyday
Some challenge more than others
How can we understand life?
And the things we encounter?

As we experience good and bad,
It seems like good never prospers
And the bad always wins
He says, "Walk away"
She says, "Forget it"
Others say, "You don't need it"
But what does one feel deep inside?

What does one say when faced with trials?
What does one say when faced with disappointments?
What does one say when faced with understatements?
What does one say when faced with disbelief and hurt?

Realize the reason why everything happens
Not always going according to plan
But according to purpose
People come
People go
But Love stays forever
Make the best of it

Mistakes are made and placed on the table
We all have sat before an imperfect plate
But judgment is best served by God alone

Step 8: Transition

    Another year managed to past leaving me with one year left in college. The summer finally came around and it was time for me to decide on the visit with my birth father. One late afternoon after work, I decided to call him and make plans for the visit.

    "Hello can I speak to John please?"

    "Sure, hold on one moment."

    As I waited for my birth father to come to the phone, I pondered over how I would begin the conversation.

    "Hello, this is John."

    "Hey, this is Meek"

    "Oh hi Meek. How have you been?"

    "I am doing pretty well. I am calling to let you know I am willing to come and visit."

    "That's great Meek. So when will it be a good time for you," he asked.

    "I was thinking maybe in a few weeks. School is just letting out for the summer so that will give me a little time off. It will be a welcomed break after being in school all year."

    "Ok that sounds great. So I will see you in a few weeks."

    Just like that, everything was settled.

    We'd agreed that I'd visit for about a week. I was still very hesitant and on the break of calling the whole thing off. All I could remember was the sting of the last visit. What if this one was the same? What if my siblings refused to accept me? Shaking myself out of my deep thoughts, I proceeded onto my daily task. The weeks went by fast and before I knew it, the time had come for me to visit my birth father. This particular time, I decided to take the bus. Man I will never do that again. That was the longest bus ride ever. It was way too much time to think. I finally arrived to my destination. As I got off the bus and waited for my birth father to pick me up, I started getting nervous all over again. My birth father arrived to pick me up along with his wife and their daughter, my stepsister. I was shocked because they actually greeted me with open arms. I was pleased to find out that my stepsister and I were very close in age. That eased my apprehension since I had someone that I could relate to while I was up here. We finally made it back to the house and my birth father showed me around and told me where I would be sleeping. After I got settled in, I called home to let everyone know I made it safely. My mother was worried about me like always, but this time I made sure she knew I would be fine.

During the visit I spent most of my time hanging out with my stepsister. John worked a lot and she made me feel really comfortable. Whenever my birth father wasn't working, we would hang out a little bit, but it was almost as awkward as being with my birth mother. I didn't know what to call him. I'd wait until we caught eye contact to start a conversation. I just couldn't bring myself to call him daddy, but I also didn't want to just call him John. I could sense that he felt just as weird as I did. One day he invited me to take a ride so that we could just be alone and talk. The silence was so palpable. Eventually we found some things to talk about and the ride didn't turn out too bad. After we got through the mounds of small talk, we got down to what we both were itching to discuss. He started off reiterating that he didn't know until late that I was his child. He kept apologizing.

"I know this must be awkward for you, I mean not knowing much about me or your birth family. I am sorry about everything. I didn't know how to break it down to my kids, your brothers and sisters. After all, it's been twenty-one years and all of a sudden we are connected with one another. Most of the family knows about your brother, Ross, but not about you. Your brother (Ross) would always tell me that I had another daughter but I didn't believe him until just recently when your mother confirmed it," my father said. I jumped in, "I don't understand. I thought you said you knew from when I was ten. Why didn't you see about me then?" None of this made sense to me. My father's response was, "Yes, your brother told me years ago, but I just didn't believe him. It wasn't until recently that your mother confirmed everything. I feel awful about the whole thing, but your mother wasn't honest with me" As I began to cry, he tried to console me and let me know that even though we just met and I was twenty-one years old, he loved me as if I've always been in his life. My heart and my ears heard conflicting tales. I wanted to believe everything and fall instantly into a father-daughter relationship, but I still resented that he didn't even check on me when he first heard of me.

We both got quiet as he drove the rest of the way back to his house. I remember glancing over at my birth father and noticed a tear or two in his eyes, but I didn't know what to say or how to say anything. I had a wealth of emotions and questions floating in my head, but like always, I swallowed them up. The truth of the matter is that I was sitting next to a stranger. I didn't know how to let those that I loved in, much less a stranger. I sat there wishing I could let him in. I wanted to love him just because he was my father, but I couldn't open my heart to the pain. When we made it back to the house, I jumped out of the car as quickly as I could. I immediately sought my stepsister. I wanted to do anything to get my mind off this heaviness. While my stepsister and I were watching TV, I overheard my birth father calling my other siblings over to the house. He explained to them that this would be my last day and he wanted them to come over and hang out with me for a little while. My siblings lived in Connecticut as well, but they stayed with their mother thirty minutes away. My brothers and sisters finally made it over. The conversation flowed, but it was evident that it was strained. My stepsister was well aware of the situation so she tried to play buffer and keep all conversations flowing. Understanding the need for us to talk privately, she excused herself after about twenty minutes. We all sat there once again trying to spark up conversation. It was very awkward and new to everyone; therefore no one really knew how to approach it. I guess this was something that could not be rushed and only time would make a difference. It was time for me to leave out for my bus so we all hugged and my birth father got ready to take me to the bus station. I made sure I said all of my goodbyes especially to my stepmother and stepsister, who made me feel more than welcomed. On the way to the bus station my father and I had one last time to talk before I went back home. I didn't feel as uncomfortable or awkward as before and I could somewhat feel the same relief from him. We pulled up the bus station. He helped me with my bags, walked me in, gave me a few dollars, and a big hug. As he walked away, I smiled giving him credit for making an attempt after finding out years later about me. He could have very well just kept it moving and never wanted to see me, but he didn't. I boarded the bus and sat down in my seat taking a deep breath for overcoming yet another painful situation. After about an hour of looking crazy, I drifted off into one of my self-to-self conversations.

  I realized things were not going to change overnight, only time would tell if things were going to get better. The second visit went far better than the first. I am happy that I went to Connecticut to see them, but if I didn't get to see them again, I'd be fine as well. I am happy to have met all of them. Perhaps that was my heart protecting itself against the expectation of having a relationship with them. I love both of my natural parents, but it's so much pain inside of me that I am unsure if I can love them the way that one should love their parents. There was an indescribable pain.

  I finally arrived back to South Carolina and boy was I happy to be home again. I wanted to start afresh, so I made a conscious decision to leave all the angst and worry on the bus. I hopped off that long bus ride feeling rejuvenated. I was ready to hang out and have a little fun. For so many years, I dwelled on my past and my situation. I really was living a 'woe is me' lifestyle. My last year in college was upon me and it was due time that I enjoyed myself.

My focus started slipping quickly. I was losing touch with myself and it was nothing anyone could do about it. I was hanging out with a few friends that happened to be at least two years younger than me. They would still be in college when I graduated in a few months. When we first met, I thought that I'd be a great role model to them. It didn't quite happen that way. Initially, I'd invite them to church and make Sunday dinner afterwards. I don't even know what happened. My grades started slipping. It was definitely by the grace of God that I graduated. When graduation came, I was so excited and ready to walk across that stage once and for all. I was so proud of myself that I'd overcome yet another thing. Everyone came to celebrate with me, even my birth father. That was a great surprise.

"I am happy you guys made it to my graduation. That means a lot me," I gushed. John seemed so proud. He said, "I would not have missed my baby girl's graduation for the world." Both of my birth mother's kids, Ross and Tam, were there. Ross was proud as well. "It is amazing how all of Momma's kids graduated from college even though she didn't play much of a role in our lives," Tam said. I thanked Tam and Ross for their congratulations, but since Tam was on the subject, I thought I'd ask about my mother. "Since we are on that subject, what happened to her coming to my graduation?" I asked. Ross was quick to offer an excuse. "She was coming, but her car broke down while she was on her way." I didn't even let him finish with that tired excuse. I just let them know that I was happy that they had come.

My mother's excuse didn't even bother me this time. I was so caught up doing my own thing. I wasn't going to let her disappoint me anymore. My father went back to Connecticut, Ross and Tam went back home and I went on with my life. I continued to hang out with my friends, but by this time I was running from everything that seemed like the right thing. I was pretending to fill out job applications during the day and at night I was hanging out heavy with my friends. I was living the life, drinking and partying all night long. I even started smoking from time to time. I knew that I wasn't doing what I was supposed to be doing, but the drinking, smoking, and partying didn't leave much time for me to dwell on what I should be doing.

From the outside looking in, I knew I was wrong. I didn't know what was going on with me. Sometimes I rationalized it by saying that nothing was wrong with having a good time. I deserved to have a good time. I had been dealt a raw hand and I still graduated. I justified it thinking that the world owed me something. I deserved a break.

I came up with all the excuses in the world, but inside I felt like garbage. I knew I had to deal with some inner demons, but I had already started running from everyone and everything. It seemed as I even ran from God.

Things were starting to get bad at home. I was staying out all night and then getting up early for work. My body was starting to shut down. I was so ashamed at my lifestyle that I started staying at a friend's house. I didn't want my mom to see me drunk and disheveled. I thought that I was keeping things from my mom, but she has such a spirit of discernment and such an ear to the Holy Spirit that she knew things that I thought I was keeping from her. It was as if someone was running to her telling her everything about me. I soon realized that it wasn't someone natural, but God Himself telling my mom all she needed to know about me. I knew I needed to return back to God, but I continued to put everything before Him. I kept Him last in my life for some time. I love that God is so patient though. Eventually, I found myself in a corner that only He could help me out of.

This one particular weekend I decided to actually stay at home. I am not sure why, but I did. That night I tossed and turned for a while and just when I thought about what I was doing wrong I also felt like it was too late. When I woke up the next morning I received a phone call from one of my closest friends whom I hung out with every day, but this time it was an unusual conversation.

"Hey Meek! Whatcha doing," said E.

"Oh nothing, just getting out of the bed. Why, what's up," I responded.

"Well when you get up, come by my house. I want to talk to you about something," E responded before hanging up.

I already knew something was up so I didn't really want to go over there. I actually remembered a few days ago how a conversation took place between me and some of our mutual friends and it didn't go too well. The conversation ended up getting back to E and it turned into one big mess. I never meant to hurt anyone or to be deceitful. I held E close to my heart, maybe too close. God gave me a great opportunity by placing some wonderful young ladies in my life for me to encourage, motivate and uplift. I didn't honor that purpose. I did the complete opposite.

Not only was something going wrong with my relationship with E, my mom finally confronted me about my recent behavior. As soon as she started talking, I began to cry. "Baby I don't know what's going on with you. I can't seem to get you to open up. At night I pray for you and during the day I worry about you. I see what's going on, even when you think I don't, but baby girl it's time for you to get it together. Meek you are twenty-three years old and it is time you make a decision about what it is you want to do. Your father and I have done all we can do, but you refuse to let us all the way in. Sometimes we feel like you don't love us the way we love you. Please talk to me and tell me what is it?" It was like my mom had wanted to say this for some time.

At that time I couldn't finish the conversation with my mother, so I asked if I could be excused. I went into my room, sat down on the bed and started thinking to myself as always. 'How did this happen? I have failed my parents, my friends don't believe me, and most of all I have turned my back once again on God. My time was up. I had failed my mission and lost focus. My parents think I don't love them the way they love me, and for some reason I have yet to conquer the task of opening up to anyone. I took a deep breath and tried to figure out my next step.

Special Tribute (Jeanette Bell, Mother)

Momma,

I was never designed from your womb
I was never given a chance to move to your tune
A man once said, count your blessings
Especially those far ahead

God heard your cry
A thousand miles away
Bringing me to you

Every night while asleep
You prayed asking God to cover me
Through a journey destined to be

Direction, guidance you instilled in me
Always there to love and care
A woman so kind and sweet
Made sure I had plenty to eat
I laugh because you never missed a beat

Getting older
Struggling into my own
Momma always picked up the phone

Time after time I heard you cry
Wondering what I felt inside
Heavy hearted with lots of pain
Don't worry momma
I am getting stronger destined to gain

God creating me to give to you
Makes life lessons durable
Even more during the course of time

Through this message
Words are invisible
Love takes the heat
Blessings are dynamic
And momma wins victory over defeat

Step 9: The Beginning Of A New Journey

Trying to clean up my act, I decided to write my parents a letter apologizing for my behavior. In the letter, I tried my best to express a few thoughts about some things that were going on within me.

Dear Momma and Daddy,

I never meant to hurt you, but sometimes we do things that only God knows why. I am so thankful for all you have done for me. When I needed someone to love me and take me in, you did just that. All these years I have tried so hard to make you proud of me, but sometimes I think I try too hard, resulting in a little disappointment. No matter how hard I try to fight my past, it just stays with me. I sometimes feel like I can't grow or move beyond my past. It's almost like a dream. I keep thinking you guys would send me away or love me less if I keep on messing up. When I open my eyes, I realize that it was just a dream because you guys have always been there and loved me. I am asking for your support, strength, and blessings as I set out to seek peace, understanding, forgiveness, strength, and responsibility within myself.

Love your baby girl,

Meek

After writing the letter, I placed it in a sealed envelope and slid it under my parents' door.

As I slid the letter under the door, I stood there for a few minutes trying to decide if I should knock. I can recall lifting my hand twice, but never actually had the courage to knock on the door. I eventually turned and walked away. As I turned and walked away I looked up and asked God to guide me on this one. I hoped that He wasn't tired of hearing from me.

Just before I actually wrote the letter, I received a phone call from one of my college friends who had moved away to Maryland after graduation. I didn't hang out with K every day, but every time we got together it was always a good time and well received. K was the type that didn't beat around the bush much, but she was always very encouraging and supportive. While we were in school, K would always tell me that she was moving to Maryland I and should come with her. I'd agree with a shrug all while knowing I had no plans to move up north to Maryland. When K moved, she called to check on me every once in a while, just to see how things were going. I could never pinpoint it, but she always showed a lot of concern for me. A bit of time had passed since we last spoke, so I guess this was our normal catching up opportunity.

"Hey Meek, what's going on with you?" she screamed across the phone. My habitual answer as always was, "nothing much, just taking it easy". K didn't miss anything. "Man it seems like every time we talk, you're taking it easy. How is everything, how is the job search," she quipped. I tried to be as vague as possible in my answer, but she wasn't going for it. She prodded and prodded until I just had to admit that things were a little hectic and I was in desperate need to make some changes. "Meek, I told you before that you needed to get out of your comfort zone. I mean it's nothing wrong with having a little fun, but you're not doing anything with yourself right now. You aren't doing anything besides stepping out of character, running from God and hurting both yourself and your parents. Tell me, is this what you imagined doing after graduating from college?" I loved that she was so direct, but yet not malicious. "No, not at all, but I guess I just got stuck," was my honest reply. "Meek it's okay. We all get like that sometimes, but now it's time for you to pull yourself together and walk your journey. I tell you what, I will put some information in the mail in the morning for you to complete. The information will include a job application and other links for employment. Make sure you complete the application and send it off no later than the end of the week. Meek, there are so many jobs available for what we received our degree in so let's take advantage of. I will call you after I put the information in the mail", said K. "Hey! K, I just want to say thank you for everything you know", I said honestly. In true K fashion, she waved me off with a, "yea yea, I know. Just like that we hung up and everything seemed a little better. I thank God that he places people in my life that seem to know exactly what to say, when to say it, and how to say it.

When I hung up the phone I started doing a little thinking about everything that has taken place thus far in my life. I knew K was right, but I had never been that far away from home for an extended time. I was very afraid. I really didn't know what I was capable of. I guess you could say I didn't have much faith in God or myself. After a day or two, I decided to give it a try. I completed the application and mailed it off. Over the course of the next week I had received a phone call requesting to schedule an interview. I was shocked and before I knew it, I had agreed to the interview. Everything was wonderful, but the interview was in Baltimore, Maryland, which just happens to be eight hours away from my home. When I got off the phone, I started spreading the news to my family. They were excited, anxious, and frightened all at once. We didn't have any family in Maryland or anywhere close to it. My mom was totally against the whole idea. She hated the idea of me possibly moving eight hours away. She didn't even want to hear anything about it.

"Meek, I don't know about you going so far away," she said. I could only rebut with the fact that she and my dad raised me well and instilled great values in me and that I would be fine. "It is my time to walk this journey and with God's guidance and your prayers, everything is going to be alright." That sounded good, but she still was very leery about it. "I still am not sure about that. I mean we don't have any family there and very little money to give you," my mother said. It was almost as if roles were reversed and I was encouraging her about all that she would normally be telling me. "Mom, don't worry about it. As you always say to me, God will work it out," I said.

The sad part about it was that I was just as nervous as my mother. I tried my best to stand there in full confidence because I didn't want my mother to notice how nervous and scared I was as well. It was time for me to step out of my comfort zone there was no better time to do it. I prayed about it over and over again, trying to make sure I was doing the right thing. I mean it was time for me to work on my faith in both God and myself, so it had to be done. Time was running out because the interview was scheduled for the following week and everything seemed to be lining up with my move. My eldest brother's best friend who had relocated to Maryland happened to be in town this weekend. My brother made a phone call and within minutes, I had a place to stay. The next step was to continue convincing my mother that I was ready to leave my comfort zone and start my new journey. Before I could blink my eyes twice I was packed up and ready to go. I was stepping out on faith getting ready for my next step. I had no idea what I was stepping into, but that was a risk I was willing to take. By this point, I was so excited and confident that I was doing the right thing. There were so many things I didn't understand, but in due time I felt like an understanding would come.

One of the things I battled with just before I left was the situation between my friends, especially E. For a long time I didn't understand why I felt so close to her or why she mattered so much to me. Maybe it was the fact that E's mom passed when she was only nine years old. She had such a good heart and only wanted a little love and attention. I felt like she was a missing piece to a part of me. I can't explain nor understand how that void really connected us. I regret that I may have ruined that sisterly relationship. I hope that one day God will give me another chance to reconnect with her and continue my mission. I pray that He would give me another chance with all of them because they were all like my little sisters. None of them believed me when I told them that I was moving away. It could be because I often told them that I was moving. They didn't believe me until they came to my house and noticed my luggage. Breezy, the sensitive one immediately started crying and begged me to stay. Tot, the most humorous one, made a joke or two and simply said that now she'd be forced to find another place to camp out during dinner. She was most like me in that she would always defer sensitive moments with a joke or off subject thing. E didn't say much, but I could tell it was bothering her as well. After we all laughed a little more, the girls went in the other room with my family. When they got up and went into the room, E stayed on the bed and that gave me a chance to speak with her.

I walked over to her and said, "I understand you are mad at me right now about everything that has taken place over the last few weeks, but believe me I never meant it. I know it may take some time for you to forgive me but always remember I love you as my own little sister." After I said that, I could tell E wanted to cry or maybe even say something back, but instead she turned her head the other way. I got up and walked into the other room with everyone else. After about another hour or so all of the girls left and it was just me and my family alone for one last night before I left.

One of the things that I loved so much about my family was when we all got together for dinner and afterwards we would sit around reminiscing and telling jokes. My oldest brother, G, was probably the funniest in our family and of course I considered myself to be the next funniest, and then my brother, Anthony. We would tell stories about how many times we got in trouble, how often my brothers got into fights, and of course how much God has blessed us over the years. At the time Anthony and G were married, G had a daughter, Te'sha and two sons, EJ and Milz. Mark's wife Madeca had just had their first child, a baby girl named Madison. My other brother Mervin also had a son, Skeeter. We laughed for hours as the kids ran around and did their normal duties of tearing my mother's house up. After about another hour, everyone decided to go home as I had to prepare for my move in the morning.

My mom had breakfast prepared for us when I woke up. It was a really emotional time for us. We all ate with tears streaming down our faces. I was sad, but still confident in my decision. I had to do this. I had to leave the nest. It even meant a lot to me that even through our tuff time, my friends sent me off with their blessings.

Once I got in the car, I didn't even want to look back. I cranked up my gospel music and got set on my long ride. I said I needed to think; nothing like eight hours on the road to allow you to think. I thought about everything while I was driving, like would I be making this move if I didn't get into that issue with my friends. I was nervous, but so proud of myself for taking such a big risk.

After what seemed like forever, I finally made it to Baltimore, Maryland. I immediately thanked God as I pulled up to my brother's best friend's house. I called my family to let them know I made it safely and also called my friend, K, to let her know that I arrived. She really didn't believe that I'd make the move. After I unpacked, I took a long shower and went right to bed.

I scared myself the next morning when I woke up and was so unfamiliar with my surroundings. It was so strange to wake up in another bed, better yet another state. Even though the sun was shining, the wind was blowing pretty hard. Coming from South Carolina, I wasn't use to this type of weather. I even turned on my heat in my Cadillac, better known as the Caddii. After I adjusted my heat and my music, I headed out to see what the city of Baltimore could offer. I was nervous about everything. There were so many cars on the road and these people were horrible drivers. My poor old school caddii could barely keep up with the traffic and the potholes. After nervously navigating through downtown Baltimore, I finally made it to my interview. I didn't know what to expect. After all, I had never been on a job interview before. It seemed like it went well, but who knows. K had planned to meet me after the interview and I was happy to see a familiar face after being in a strange city.

"Hey! Meek, you made it," she squealed. "Girl, you didn't tell me it would be such a long drive," I replied. Just like her, she said, "Now you see why I don't make it back home that often. So how did the interview go?" I really didn't know, but they told me that they would let me know within a week. I was really excited to see K. We talked about everything as we headed to her cousin's house.

K's cousin, Nida, lived in Baltimore, but was from South Carolina like the rest of us. She was very intelligent and helpful. She seemed to know a lot about searching for a job and she gave me some very useful information. She greeted me as if she had already met me. She said K told her some great things about me. It's great to meet people that give you such a welcoming embrace. I had a good feeling about her and about my move.

Nida helped me to apply for several other jobs. I was even able to secure another interview for the next day. After what seemed to be a productive afternoon, I headed back to my brother's best friend's house. He lived in the Glen Burnie area, which was at least thirty-five minutes from civilization. There were things in Glen Burnie, but everything worthwhile was at least a half hour away. On my drive, I received another call back from a company and was asked to come in the next morning. The interview went well and I was offered the job on the spot for a position working with troubled youth. It was amazing how fast things were coming together.

My intentions were only to stay with my brother's friend for a short while. He had a family and I didn't want to be an inconvenience. They never made me feel unwelcome, but I didn't want to overstay my welcome either. Nida had an apartment that she shared with her two sisters and two other roommates. K lived with her uncle, but was also looking to move. K and I thought it would be a good idea if we roomed together so that we could both save some money. For a short while, we moved into Nida's already cramped apartment. It was a sight to see all of us trying to get ready for work. Six females trying to use one bathroom was a struggle all in itself. Somehow, we made it work. It was as if we knew the bathroom and shower schedule and stayed in tune with it.

I was on my grind working hard and trying my best not to get home sick or think about my sticky situation with my friends back home. I tried to call E a few times, but she didn't accept my phone calls. I did get a chance to speak with Breezy and TD, but it was very brief. I was actually quite busy and rarely had time to call them anyway. Out of the blue one day, I received a call from one of my biological brothers, Ross.

Hello

Hey Meek what's up?

Nothing much, just trying to get myself together up here in this big city.

I hear that. So tell me, do you like it so far?

Well it's only been a little over a month, so I am still trying to find my way around. Everything is good with me. How are you doing brother?

Well I was calling because I am thinking about relocating up there too.

What! When did you, no, what made you decided that?

Well, one, I always wanted to leave from down south, and two you know my girl is in the military up there.

Ok well just keep me posted and let me know what's good. How soon are you looking to come up?

Probably within the next month or so, but I will let you know.

All right. I will talk to you later.

My birth brother and I exchanged numbers back when I graduated from college and kept in contact ever since. We didn't speak too often, but often enough. Ross' girlfriend was in the military at the time and stationed here in Maryland. His plan was to move up here and live with her. He originally told me that he'd let me know within a month, but that month turned into two weeks. He decided to move up to Maryland.

Ross moved up here without any idea of how it is to live on a military base. He wanted to hang out late and drink and behave all kinds of ways, but that kind of behavior was not tolerated on the military base. Needless to say, his girlfriend did not take too kindly to Ross' behavior or the idea of her getting kicked off of the military base. When posed with the ultimatum, his girlfriend wisely chose the military over a relationship with Ross. Now Ross was here in Maryland with no girlfriend, but more importantly, with no place to stay. Even though he and I were not too close, I could not stand to see my brother homeless in a strange place. I was uncomfortable doing so, but I prepared myself to ask Nida to allow him to stay in her already cramped place until he or I could find a place of our own.

I tried to explain the situation to Nida as best as I could. I said a silent prayer before I came to her with the outlandish idea. "Hey Nida, I need a favor. If you can't do it, I understand." I tried to give her an out, but really hoped that she wouldn't take it. "What is it Meek," she calmly replied. I tried to find the best way to say, "Well my brother, Ross, moved up here to stay with his girlfriend, but that fell through and he's stuck right now. He needs a place to stay." Nida understood and offered him some floor space. Like me, she couldn't stand to see him on the street and knew that the other housemates wouldn't have a problem with another person in the house. I was so thankful and I let her know that I hoped to be out and in my own place within the next couple of weeks.

We were tight in our two-bedroom apartment, but we made it work. As I hoped, K and I finally received word about getting our own apartment. We moved into our place that same week. This move has been an ordeal, but by the grace of God, I survived. We didn't have any furniture, so we borrowed Nida's air mattress. We used most of our money to secure the apartment, but we were able to save just enough to buy the necessary groceries. As we unpacked the groceries, we laughed and reminisced about our past meager living arrangements.

"Hey Meek, do you remember when we had to sit outside for a while before going into that small two-bedroom apartment?"

"Man, K that was crazy. There were six of us living in there. Well now we have a place of our own," I commented. "God is so good. I don't know how we made it, but we did. "

K jumped in, "Isn't Ross supposed to be bringing our furniture?"

"We don't have any furniture, but he is supposed to help us move our clothes," I laughed.

We settled in nicely as the days went by. Everything was set and in place with the apartment. The only thing that we needed to do was buy furniture, but we'd buy some piece by piece as we could afford it. We weren't too far from Nida's apartment, so we had easy access to all of the necessities that we didn't have at our own place. Ross crashed on our couch for a couple of weeks. He even was able to secure a job with the same organization that I worked at. Living and working with him was odd. For a large portion of our life, we didn't know each other. We were connected by blood, but there was still a disconnection between us. Having reconnected in our adult lives, both of us were set in our ways and accustomed to our other familial relationships. It was a task to build a relationship with him, but we were trying. We were similar in some ways, but in others, we were drastically different. My problem with Ross was that he was very inconsiderate and always felt like everybody owed him something. I didn't bring it to his attention often, but one day, I'd had enough.

"Ross, I don't understand why you always feel like everybody owes you something," I said. He was taken aback, but he responded honestly. "I mean Meek, you don't know what it's like to not have someone to call on because you always had Mervin, Jeanette, Anthony, G, and Dee to call on if you needed something," he complained. I was immediately offended and fired back, "Oh ok so that's what this is all about. Because you think that I was raised so perfectly you can take advantage of me?" I didn't realize that I started to cry, but as tears streamed down my face, I continued. "Let me tell you something. Never judge a book by its cover. My parents worked hard, they struggled, we struggled, just like any other family, but through it all we had love to hold us up. So don't blame me for who you are or for what you don't have." Neither of us was considering the other's feeling. He quickly shot back with "well Meek, you and Tam had somebody to help out with everything. I had to work hard for what I needed ever since I was a child". I felt no sympathy. "Ross, at least you and Tam had a chance to know what it's like to live with our mother, even if it was only for a short time. Not only did you guys get to live with her, you guys got to live with each other; you got to live with your sister. Besides that, you also were able to know and have relationship with our father. So please don't give me the 'woe is me' speech. You got everything that I needed, and longed for from our parents. How do you think it feels to believe that no one that shares your own blood wants anything to do with you? So yes, I was blessed to have a great mother and father, but it will never change that desire to want it from my birth and you had that."

Just before we could finish our conversation K walked in the house and I got up and went into my room.

Hey! Meek is everything alright K said, I am alright (as the tears rolled down my face). I mean either you like crying or something is wrong with you K said. I just don't understand I try my best to do something good but once again my past just will not let me go I said. Let me guess you and your brother got into an argument? K said. Yes he seems to blame me for being blessed with a family that was able to take care of me; I don't get it he had the chance to be around our mother father, and family throughout his life. I wasn't given that opportunity but yet it's my fault I said. Meek you can't let that bother you, I know it's easy for me to say that but look around you are blessed. God found a family that could love you as if you were there own. Understand your brother hurts just like you but he have different ways of dealing with it and I believe in due time you guys will find a way to get it right K said. Thanks K anytime Meek K said as she got up and walked out of the room. After K walked out of the room I got up off the bed and prepared myself for work.

While driving to work I started thinking about how fast time was moving and I was starting to really get used to being in Baltimore. It was around my third month and that's when I notice a little change in my life. Working with the youth listening to some of the things they experience in life at such young ages took me back in my past a little. I mean these teens were in some difficult situations, some far more advance than my own. All those times I spent crying about being abandon I never took the time to realize how blessed I was to have a family that loved and cared for me. I spent more time being selfish than thankful. Some of these kids never had a chance to experience love or anything close to it. Every day was different than the last working with the youth. Through the trying times I developed great relationships with them allowing them to open up and share their feelings with me. It took me a while to understand but I finally realized that working with the youth was truly a passion and it allowed me to grow as an individual.

I found myself reaching out to my family more especially my mother. Ever since I found out about my situation I allowed myself to pull back. I didn't know how to talk to my mother anymore. The move to Baltimore along with my job allowed me to appreciate my family even more. I always wanted that relationship with my mother but never knew how to get it. I started to take one day at a time reaching out, calling home weekly just to express my love and appreciation. I was excited about my journey and the new things I was started to experience but of course this was only the beginning. I could tell that I was starting to get a little comfortable and that wasn't a good thing for me.

After a while I started meeting new and excited people around my age group from work and we started hanging out. My gospel collection fell off the chart while R&B Rap took over. It was like a repeat all over again. I was living the life, making money, hanging out, drinking and partying all night long after work. Of course I met other individuals (positive) that tried to help me at least keep a balance but that didn't work, I didn't want a balance. The only thing I thought about was doing what I wanted whenever I wanted to do it. I would work during the day motivating, guiding, and showing leadership to the youth, while at night I was living the life. I mean I was becoming a young adult and after working all day I wanted to have a little bit of fun. I was twenty three years old, finally away from home and free to do whatever I wanted. I was living in another state with things I had never seen before and I wanted to see what Baltimore had to offer.

A year went by and my birth brother finally moved out into his own apartment. We (my birth brother and I) were learning how to work on our relationship by reaching out to one another. It took us sometime but after a while we started realizing how much we really needed each other. K and I eventually moved in a much bigger apartment in the same complex as my birth brother and man that was a huge come up. We were making enough money to furnish the apartment and buy other little things we needed to make our apartment feel like a home. We started getting our shop on and of course K had to help me with my shopping. I was always somewhat of a tomboy who played sports and thought wearing heals and dressing up was too much, but one day I gave it a try huh! That was the day the men starting coming. I was stepping out, looking good the guys were on my heels, and I loved it. I was excited about going out and meeting new people, especially the men.

After a while I started to create even more problems for myself, by trying to fill the empty spaces in my life with lust from men. Growing up I watched how my brothers dated and even helped them tell lies so of course I thought I had the game all figured out. I had a chance to see it from a different point of view. One thing I forgot about the most was getting that mother daughter talk about the things I didn't learn from watching my brothers; you know the things you need a woman's advice about. Don't get me wrong it had nothing to do with my mother not being there but it had all to do with me shutting her out of my life. My mother was the sweetest lady you would ever want to meet but at the same time she didn't play with us at all. I guess it was a mixture of me dealing with my past situation along with being afraid to open up and talk to her so I learned a few things the hard way. I was talking to a few guys here and there not really wanting to settle down but just enjoying the moments. I found myself doing things I had never done before but I was too afraid to talk with my mother and ashamed to talk with my friends because of course I was like the late bloomer. I spent so much time being a tomboy until I was out of the loop if that's what you want to call it. I was all over the place but I did a good job trying to cover it up. After a while I slowed down on my calling home every day because I was getting into too much at once. I didn't want my mother to know her precious little girl was lusting behind men and hanging out all night. In my head all I could think about was being my mother's little girl and nothing else. It was almost like I was never supposed to grow up and experience life. I guess a lot of the blame was my fault but that was something I didn't realize at the time. It was crazy I mean every time I felt like a guy wanted to get too close I was ready to jump ship. I started getting confused about what I wanted and what I deserved. I even lost track of knowing what I was worth and decided to lower my standards enough to settle. All that talk about thinking I knew by watching my brothers was the wrong approach. I mean I wasn't stupid by a long shot but it was also a lot I had yet to learn. This part of my life was just beginning but we will talk a little more on that later down the line.

    A few months later another classmate moved up from South Carolina to live with me and K. We all were like family me, my brother, K and Lee-lee. Lee-lee and K were actually friends while in college. I never really knew Lee-lee until she moved up. I was able to get her a job working with troubled youth at the same agency I worked for and she started hanging out with my friends and I. Life was good I mean I had a good job, new friends, money, and I also had the chance to make things right with my friends from home. We were hanging out every chance we could. We even started traveling to different states and countries, man it was great being single and lusting all at the same time. I never allowed myself too much time alone because I knew that would give me time to think about all the things I was getting myself into. Lee- lee had finally moved out into her apartment but we were still hanging strong. I would stay over her side of town at least four days out of the week. She actually moved down the street from our job so it was very convenient for me to get to and from work. We partied together so much it became our middle name. It was so serious that my brother and I had a party each year for our birthday being that they were only one day apart (but we were three years apart). We would entertain and get everybody drunk all at the same time. If we were throwing a party everyone knew that was the place to be, huh! Especially if you wanted to laugh, get drunk, and just have some good old fun. I was having so much fun until I had lost touch with going to church or even taking the time out to pick my bible up for a quick read. I was lost and refused to deal with my inner self as long as I could; drinking, hanging out, and lusting for male companionship had become a part of my everyday life style and I was comfortable with doing just that. I was running fast. Whenever someone said Meek you wanna go, before they could get it all out I was like sign me up. I moved to Baltimore when I was twenty three going on twenty four and I ran this race for as long as time allowed me too. It was almost like I had to be everywhere at all times without skipping a beat. I guess I was finally getting the feel of what it was like being on your own. Things were going real good but this one particular day I decided to stay home for a little while mainly because I was tired and needed a little rest. K came in the house and sat down beside me on the chair. I already knew what time it was when she sat down but I just waited for her to say something.

    What's up Meek? K said, nothing much K how about with you? I said. Oh nothing just working hard that's all. Let me ask you something K said, go ahead I said. (I could have said no but huh! That wasn't going to stop K, if she had something to say you better believe it was going to be said). How long are you going to keep doing this to yourself? What are you talking about I said, let me ask you again how long are you going to keep doing this to yourself. I don't know what you are talking about K but I gotta go so I will talk to you later I said.

One thing was for sure and that was K knew me better than any of my friends at the time. She knew that I was running and caught up in something I didn't have enough strength to get out of. K was not the most perfect individual but she knew enough to recognize what was going on. I honestly believe God placed us together for a reason and it would come to pass sooner than later. I was back at it again trying my best to keep up with the life I was living. Another year past by this time K and I had been in our new apartment for a year and half and we were doing really well.

Of course I was still with the youth but I was given an opportunity to work with the older kids 14-21 years of age. I tell you what, that was a true eye opener for me. I was working with (young teenagers). They really looked up to me. When I came into work I actually made a difference in their lives. It was a wonderful yet sad experience all at the same time. The wonderful part was being able to develop relationships, teach them responsibility, guidance, and gain such great experience. Whenever I saw the smile on their faces it made my heart reach another level of happiness. I don't know. It was something about working and reaching out to those kids. The sad part is I was dealing with teenagers who never really knew what it was like to have someone to take time out to listen, and show concern. These kids had been from group home to group home and could see right through you, if you didn't have their best interest trust me they could tell. I had a natural bond with those kids and I took my job seriously, don't get me wrong, I have had my times to where I wanted to walk away because being in the human service field can have a serious drain on a person. It was like a dream, you know, you had youth who never knew any of their parents, youth being abuse by their parents (verbal, physical, sexual), and youth who parents just walked away in the middle of the night. This was something I was definitely not used to but I tried my best not to let it show. They always seem to have some excuse as to why they couldn't do this or that, huh! It always had something to do with what they had been through. They would be quick to say (you don't know what I been through, so you can't tell me anything). The teenaged girls were doing any and everything under the sun with both genders, all because they either saw it done before or just never had anyone to teach them right from wrong. They were letting young and older men take advantage of them and boy was I not happy with that, but in this field we are taught never to take it personal.

Some of the things I heard from them in reference to men/young boys made my little honeymoon with men look like cupcakes. I knew at that time I had to crack down and teach them what I had and was still learning at the time. It wasn't about being personal to me but more so being a help, providing some hope, and guidance. No one ever really took the time out to teach them therefore they were following the footsteps of peers, or steps of what they saw on the streets. Man! And let me to tell you the things they saw, scratch that the things I saw on the streets of B-More in the city were steps a sista was scared to embrace. School went from being an option to being a choice; if those kids attempted to go to school they could pass. I mean at least that's what it seems like to me, because the grades those kids brought home were horrible, but for some odd reason they still passed to the next grade. It was almost like the teachers said Oh! You're in a group home; as long as you make an attempt you pass the class. On the other hand you had teachers who treated them bad/or different just because they were in a group home. If you ask me, both ways were not good. While working with the teenagers I tried to teach them to work hard for what they want, don't just accept anything. I found myself teaching them life skills such as: how to clean up, how to cook, how to study, respect, responsibility, and how to complete a job application. I embraced every task they completed, every smile on their faces, and every chance I had to make a difference.

Throughout the same year I had received a promotion on my job as a supervisor and that meant more money (laugh out loud). It meant more money (not that much) but it also meant I had to relocate down to another site. I was sad and believe me the youth I was working with went crazy (figure of speech). I was a bit hesitant at first because I was somewhat attached to the group I was working with but the new position brought about some good as well. It gave me a chance to work with another wonderful group of teenagers, flexibility, and a greater level of experience. The flexibility worked because I was able to go home more often and visit with my family. I took full advantage of it every time. I would go home and listen to my mother tell me how proud of me they were and how much they missed me. My brothers G and Anthony always said WE LOVE YOU SIS NOW GET MONEY. They were business men who always found ways to make money. It always felt so good to be home with my family because over the years I realized the true value of family. Living in Baltimore and working with different children/people I notice family was not as much of a priority. The majority of the parents didn't care about raising their kids and most of the time you had children trying to raise children. I know that happens all over the world but this was all new to me and it took me by surprise. I guess it was because I didn't get out much until my moved to Baltimore.

My new position changed some things for me a little bit. My hours were different meaning Lee-lee and I no longer had the same days off and with me being a supervisor I had to change up some things in my professional outlook. I found myself staying home a bit more I wasn't really sure why but I guess it was something that just happened. One day while I was at home watching television in my room there was a knock at the door.

Knock, knock, who is it I said, its K come in buddy I said. How are you doing Meek K said, I am doing alright just hanging in there that's all. So have you decided on how long you are going to keep doing this to yourself K said? K you know the funny thing is I ask myself the same thing every day but nothing changes. I have been running so long until I don't know what to do. We'll Meek maybe it's time you stop faking the funk. Everybody has different timing and callings on their life and yours is now but you don't want to face it. You are blessed to have a great gift for helping people and working with children don't miss out on what God has for you. I don't know when my time will be but I do know yours is here and you may need to get serious about it K said. Maybe your right but for now let's just enjoy the rest of this movie I said.

I knew exactly what K was saying but it was something I was just not ready to deal with. It's funny because until my move to Baltimore, I never really even knew what I was capable of doing. Anyway I said to myself I just want to finish this movie without putting thought into anything else.

Over the course of the next two years things started changing once again. I was offered a job with another agency and decided to take it (again more money). During this time Lee-lee was in a serious relationship and I didn't see much of her or any of my other friends due to changing jobs. I had actually changed jobs at least twice that year. I was starting to realize my steps were getting shorter and I was eager to find my inner self. I was spending more time with myself and less time with others. I decided to start visiting churches a little here and there but no promises were made. The following year I finally picked up a job that had nothing to do with my field of study. Things started to change in my life as I struggled within daily. I was confused about these changes because of course I didn't authorize them but what was I going to do about it. I went from partying all the time to barley even going out at all. I thought I was going to lose my mind, I mean I actually had to spend time alone. Of course when I was younger I spent a lot of time by myself but that was years ago. It was almost like I was in another world alone, and I was forced to spend time with myself (which increased my talk time to myself). After about a few months I started back working out to keep myself a little busy. I would talk to Lee-lee every once in a while but not enough for us to actually hang out. I had a very hard time excepting what was happening but again what was I going to do about it. I was kinda going through the motions for about another year before the truth hit the fan. I was on a journey and everything I had been dealing with and going through was only making me stronger, responsible, and self-sufficient. I was trying to become my own person and not what everyone else wanted me to be at that time. My work experience, and everyday life style was teaching and molding me. All this time I thought God had left me but he never did, instead he allowed me to go through my every moment just as planned. Every situation from drinking, partying, hanging out, and lusting were all made by me. I always felt like I had to fit in and I was willing to lower my standards to do so. I put so much thought into other people until I forgot who and what it was like to be me; honestly I was just starting to find myself. This was like the beginning all over again and I had to take another step forward. Once again I had started back talking to my mother almost on a daily basis and it was a wonderful thing. It was wonderful because I started to express myself, about me. Of course I didn't open up totally all at once but it was a work in progress. Another thing I realized over the course of the next few months was by me complaining, I wasn't getting anywhere. I decided to minimize my complaining, instead I started smiling and enjoying my time alone. It was actually fun because I started discovering things about myself and my surroundings I never knew. I even made the best of my job although it wasn't something I really enjoyed like that. I was used to working with the youth and this job had nothing to do with youth. I mean don't get me wrong, I was able to work with older (adult) students but it wasn't the same. I had to sit at my desk calling students trying to get them to enroll in school and that was for the birds. I was down for people going back to school but I wasn't trying to force nobody to sign up if they didn't want to do it. Anyway this one particular day while at work sitting at my desk making phone calls, I stumbled across a very unfamiliar name and number. I was thinking to myself what kind of name is Naomi, I started to skip it because I could barely pronounce it. I thought to myself man, let me just call this girl. I picked up the phone and dialed her up, and she answered the phone. We started talking about her going back to school for a hot second then I skipped the subject; I was good for that (skipping the subject). I started asking her other questions about what she does for a living and cracking jokes. One thing about me I loved to laugh and make others laugh. Well the conversation went a little like this Naomi happened to be a young lady around my age which was twenty six at the time, she had a vision. She had a vision to uplift, motivate, and inspire, young African American women. Her mission was to provide, create, nurture, and maintain a positive environment of growth, challenges, and unlimited possibilities for every woman who desires it. After finding that information out I forgot why I called her but I knew I wanted to know more. Naomi emailed me some information and opened her organization up for me to come to one of their gatherings. We exchanged numbers while on the phone, along with me excepting an invitation to visit her church. After a while I had to get off the phone, if I still wanted my job. It was clear that our conversation had nothing to do with me enrolling students.

A few days later Naomi contacted me and invited me to one of their monthly gatherings. During the gathering I was able to meet several other positive black women destined to gain. I thought to myself maybe this was what I needed? I also attended Naomi's church all in the same week. I must admit that was a pretty good week. After about a few more visits with the organization and Naomi church I decided to join them both. I was excited about both the organization and the church; I even invited one of my good friends Eb (co-worker) at the time to come out to the gatherings. I was spreading the word and wanted everyone to get involved with such a positive organization. Two of my other good friends joined as well (Tash & Nikki). Things in my life were happening so fast until I couldn't believe my eyes. I started spending more time with the young ladies within the organization, especially Naomi which was the president and Kenu the vice president. Naomi was the preacher's daughter of the church I joined. She was very different but wise at the same time. Kenu on the other hand was very funny and easy going. She was dedicated to the organization and still found time to spend with her wonderful husband. Eventually I accepted an officer position as (Membership Liaison) due to one of our other members stepping down. I was taking on more responsibility but I was cool with it. I was doing positive things, attending church, and working but something was still missing. I was experiencing this pulling feeling within but I kept trying to ignore it.

Anyway my 27th birthday was approaching and a celebration was in preparation. As I mention earlier every year since my birth brother and I lived in Baltimore we celebrated our birthday together. We would have one party at his house and go out to celebrate on the next night. This particular year for some reason I wasn't too pumped about parting for our birthdays. I mean I wanted to celebrate them but I didn't really feel up to going all out. I knew how much my brother wanted this party, especially with it being his 30th birthday so I went along with it. I was trying my best to enjoy the night but it was hard. I had all of my friends there, even Lee-lee whom I had not seen in a while. It was really good to see her after all this time, it felt a little different I guess because we hadn't seen each other for a minute. We laughed, danced, drank, and celebrated the night away. Throughout the night it was like I was forcing myself to have fun, not because I wasn't happy but I just couldn't get rid of that heavy pulling. Friday and Saturday was finally over and I was free to go home and rest after two days of laughter, excitement, and fun with family/friends. Sunday after church I came home, ate dinner, and prepared myself for the next working day. Before going to bed that night I spoke with my mother as usual, while talking to her I was trying to explain the feeling I was having for over the last month or so. I told her it was like a pulling from within but I just couldn't put my finger on it. Of course my wonderful mother told me to pray about it, she was just so excited to see me back in church and keeping myself busy. Sometimes I think my mother knew that I was going through my little phases but she just allowed me to work through it on my own. I guess she felt like in due time I would pull myself together.

After spending half of the night tossing and turning, it was Monday morning before I knew it. I pushed my way into work that morning but I was still dealing with that heavy pulling and it was getting worst. I made it through the day and while on my way home I notice that the air appeared to feel a little dryer than usual. I finally arrived home, got out of the car and headed up the steps to my apartment. While walking up the steps I notice a sudden rush from head to toe causing me to grasp the dry air as the pulling continued. When I went into the house I decided to pull out one of my favorite gospel CD, s and jam to it for bit. I was standing in my bedroom when I felt another sudden rush in my body, the music seemed louder and the pulling transitioned outward causing me to drop down on my knees. Tricking no one but me the tears began to roll down my face, my hands started to shake, my feet were sweating, my knees were in pain, and my pulling had caused an inner explosion that had manifested for over twenty something years.

I can remember it like it was yesterday. It was the night of January 9, 2007. I was sitting on the floor in front of my dresser as the radio played my favorite gospel CD's over and over again I finally gave in. Opening up to God the words started to flow, giving up all of me. Asking God to take away anything that was not like him. Crying continuously reaching out to him after hiding for over twenty or more years, I wanted to be free from hurt, conviction, the feeling of being alone, hatred, and the lack of loving myself the way God loved me. All this time I ran away from really getting to know God, I was afraid of having a relationship with (God). When he isolated me, he was trying to get my attention, when he placed me in a job that had nothing to do with my experience it was for his reason. It was a time for change within me and I had to start by developing a relationship with God. I spent practically all my life in church, but most of the time I was going through the motions. Don't get me wrong I always believed in God but never took the time out to actually have a relationship with him for myself. When I was younger I pointed a lot of fingers and blaming on others (including God) until it was impossible to have any type of relationship.

This journey is guiding me to a greater understanding within myself, my past, my present, my future, and most importantly with God. Of course after making a decision to live and long for a relationship with God I had to pay a price. The price wasn't going to be easy but through this journey I would experience an even greater understanding/love for God.

Step 10: In search of my purpose while on this Journey

Monday morning I got up and went into work feeling good. I was smiling from ear to ear and pumped about sitting at my desk all day for once. I walked over to my desk and logged in my phone and went to work. Around lunch time my supervisor came over to remind me about our regularly scheduled meeting for that evening. He mentioned to me on his way out that his supervisor would be sitting in on the meeting as well. After he walked away I thought to myself that it was a little crazy, I mean he has never sat in any of our meetings before. I shook it off and continued what I was doing, for some reason I wasn't worried about it. Finally the time came for us to meet and I went into the office. The meeting went well at least for me, because I was finally able to speak my mind (in a professional way of course) but I guess it was too much of the truth. The day was over and on my way out I felt a really funny feeling almost as if that day was my last day. Well it was, shortly after I got off from work my supervisor called apologizing for what he was about to say.

Hello Shameka I am so sorry he said, about what I said. Well unfortunately my supervisor wasn't pleased with your comments during the meeting and felt like your services were no longer needed within our agency. He said I am sorry, I tried whatever I could do to get him to reconsider. Please let me know if it is anything I can do to be of assistance. Shameka you were a wonderful employee with such motivation, dedication, and drive. I know that where ever you go, you will succeed and accomplish greatness. I said in return thank you, and don't worry about me I am going to be just fine. My time was up here and now I must go forward in search of my purpose.

After hanging up the phone I took a few minutes to just tell God thank you, as I proceeded in the direction of bible study. I will admit I did drop a tear or two but I knew everything was going to be alright. By this time I was actually attending bible study during the week and church on Sunday's, I was excited about this new relationship I was establishing with God. When I finally got home that night I sat down on the bed and a voice said to me, finish what you started. I didn't understand at first but I heard it again, finish what you started. This is your time, to finish what you have started. I started thinking about all the things I started or wanted to do but I was a bit lost at first. I got up off the bed and started looking into my closet and while I was standing there my bag feel on the floor. I picked the bag up and some papers fell out of a notebook, when I open the notebook I notice some work I had started a while back but never finished. A few years ago God had laid it on my heart to write about my story, at first I thought to myself, me writing that's not happening. I received another conformation from my Pastor (Antonio Gathers) at my home church in South Carolina stating the same thing. When I moved to Maryland I played around with my writing here and there a few times but again nothing serious. I guess I was so caught up in having fun until I ignored the feeling of writing.

Anyway when I picked up the notebook of my writing I heard a voice say again now finish what you started. I started thinking back to everything that had taken place in my life thus far and just couldn't believe it. I was finally at a point where I was forced to finish what I started. I didn't have a choice everything was taken away from me my job to my social life. God had isolated me again but this time it was me and him. It was crazy because my cell phone stopped ringing, and I found myself spending even more time either in church, with the organization, talking on the phone with my mother, or home writing. I went from having a few male friends to having none at all. I also spent time searching for jobs but for a while that wasn't successful, so I continued to write. I was not only getting closer to God but I was getting even closer to my mother and that was a wonderful feeling.

Every week it was the same thing during the day I would read my bible, sing a few songs, and write. I mean it was actually a good feeling, because the more I wrote the more I found myself, God, and forgiveness. The more I wrote the more I wanted to know, so I finally set aside my stubborn ways and opened back up to my birth mother. I actually listened to her tell me some of the things she battled with, dealt with and lived with during her life. Listening to her talk made me kind of understand a little more as to why I was always afraid to commit or even get close to anyone. My birth mother was married before and dated around a lot. I mean it was still so many things I didn't know about her but it was a work in progressed. Some things I may never find out, but that's something I will just have to live with. She apologized for everything, but we both knew that a relationship was probably not going to happen. I don't think I could ever see her as a mother but more like a friend. I was able to forgive but I am still learning how to love her beyond my pain.

As I continued to write, the tears rolled down my face, my heart got heavy, and my pain fell through my chest. I felt like I was living in my past but this time I was gaining a little bit of understanding and forgiveness at the same time. When I think about the youth and things they actually go through my heart goes out because I know what it's like to never forget or use your past to slow down your present/future. I joked about writing but the more I encountered through the youth and other individuals the more I heard God's voice telling me to write. The entire time I had been going through the motions living and learning I realized this was something that I had to do. I was set out to inspire, motivate, encourage, and strengthen many through what was given, introduced, taught, and experienced by God, myself, and others. I was excited about writing and sharing with others but I didn't realize how much work it was or even what was yet to come while on this journey.

 I continued to search for jobs and write during the day. I was living on cloud nine, God was making a way for my bills to get paid, I was enjoying my relationship with him, and church was my number one place to be. I had stopped really hanging out to clubs, bars, and I even stopped drinking. When things got tight God blessed me with a job right on time, I mean you couldn't tell me anything. My job was back working with the youth (my passion) and I was still going to church strong, things were alright. I was content with not having a male companion in my life because I knew if I was doing right God would bless me with my husband (ya I said it). I was ready to commit for the very first time in my life. I was practicing abstinence and everything; I was well on my way to the perfect Christian girl (huh!). Well again I was hanging in there but this one particular day a young man from the church approached me shortly after service. He was a very nice looking young man; I had noticed him for a while but never said anything out of the way. I was working on this new thing where I wanted the guy to approach me, not me always going after what I wanted. He approached me, we talked, laughed and it was actually pretty cool. He asked for my number I gave it to him and we started chatting a little here and there. He knew all about me trying to wait until marriage for sex, he knew all about me attending church often and wanting to have a relationship with God. He was cool with it, because he was trying to do the same thing. After that I knew he was a keeper, we got along so well. Time went on and I actually decided to tell my parents about him and ask if I could bring him home with me one weekend. I think I shocked the entire town when I said that because I never brought anyone home. I was always so busy running whenever the guy would get too close they never stood a chance. This guy was on his way to getting close. He was very patient with me and seemed to understand me so well. Anyway the time came for him to go home with me and that was the test. Just before we got ready to go down south I noticed so many red flags but I kept trying to look passed them. I mean he was going to meet my parents, I guess that mean I thought he could have been the one for me. Well once we got down south more red flags appeared, my mother pulls me to the side and I could tell in her eyes she wasn't really with it. I think we both knew and felt the same thing. The weekend went by fast and now it was time for us to head back to Maryland. While driving I started thinking about the conversation I had with my mother, along with my personal thoughts and feelings. I realized that I never referred to him as my boyfriend but just as a friend. I always felt like friend was a better choice. It made me feel a little less committed. When we arrived back to Maryland I dropped him off and went home. I few days went by with no contact from him. It seemed a bit strange but I didn't spend too much time dwelling on it. During those few days I continued to pray about the relationship, I wanted and needed conformation. Days later I found out the real deal behind my friend. He had a few habits like drinking and cheating that manage to surface. He stopped attending church and said to me I can finally be me. I thought to myself well, who were you before? It was hard for me to swallow; I even thought I could change him but I found out you can't change a person unless they are willing to make the changes themselves. My mother had to help me through the situation because I couldn't understand. I know I saw those flags and felt what my mother felt but I thought well he is in church, how could I go wrong? I thought he was the one, do you hear me? It took me a minute to grasp what was taking place, between the pastor and my mother I had no choice but to grasp it. I was mad because I thought I was doing something right, for the first time I allowed him to get close to me. I am not saying that he wasn't a nice guy but just not for me. He wanted me to accept something's I just wasn't willing to accept and I realized trying to change a person that doesn't want to be change is a waste of time. I wonder to this day if he's still involved in drugs and alcohol, or even if he considered change. I am thankful; of course it took me a minute to realize that I could have been in a regretful situation. I tell you what God worked in my favor and redirected my steps out of the situation.

 A month later my grandmother passed away and I was back home (South Carolina) dealing with one of the hardest things in my life and that was watching my mother cry. My grandmother was a legend of her times, a mighty woman of God, who loved her grand and great grandkids dearly. The death of my grandmother was hard but I had to be strong for my mother who happens to be the oldest out of four siblings. Overcoming another obstacle I returned to Maryland. I was actually a little excited because I was offered another job as a Family Service Coordinator and upon my return I accepted the offer. I continued to work at my current job as a Life Skills Specialist because I enjoyed working with them. Throughout my years of working with the youth I often found myself not being able to walk out on them so easily. I guess it has a lot to do with understanding what it's like to feel abandoned

Around this time I had discovered some issues within my current ministry and after praying about it I decided to leave the church. It was hard for me because I really found myself gaining strength and learning more about God within this ministry. After leaving the ministry I continued my search for another ministry to fellowship with.

T.D. Jakes mention something in one of his books (Six Pillars from Ephesians) that best describes how I feel at times. He said Pastors, teachers, prophets, evangelists-all who function in roles of authority in the church- must admonish God's people with the same attitude as a loving father in the home. Those who provoke their congregations to wrath by man-made teaching and man-made rules that are harsher than God's Law are going to find they are rising up angry, harsh people. We are to win the worlds through the manifested strength and power of God's love, not the strength and power of men and women seeking to build their own empires.

Times have changed and ministry just isn't what it was a long time ago at least not to me. After a few months of searching and trying to stay focused I finally found another church to fellowship with thanks to a good friend of mine Kynu. It was her old church by the name of Kingdom Builders Worship Center. The ministry appeared to be a really nice ministry and I enjoyed attending the church. I don't know, I think somewhere down the line I felt myself losing the motivation for attending church. I also felt myself falling back from my relationship with God. I started getting comfortable in hanging out and having a little fun. After a while I was back into some of my old ways again. The summer months were approaching and it was time for me to go home (down south) to visit my family for the summer. By this time I wasn't thinking about finishing my book just having fun. I don't know several times I thought to myself why are you even trying to write a book? Who wants to hear about my story especially when everybody is writing about his/her personal life now days? I was finally home in South Carolina excited as I could be especially since I had already had it in my head that I was going to be moving back down south within the next few months. I was happy about that; after all I had been trying to move back down south for the last two years. I had been praying about it for what seemed like forever and I was finally going to be moving closer to my family leaving the city behind me. Anyway I was home spending time with my family, and friends just having a great time. I even had the opportunity to attend my 10 year class reunion and what a great time that was. I got the chance to see Nicole my (my middle school best friend), and a few other old friends. Huh! It was like old times almost man, I really did miss Nicole. Anyway the majority of the girls I didn't get along with in high school turned out to be real cool and laid back. We all had such a wonderful time and I never knew they were that cool. Oh yes let me not forget I had the chance to see my high school sweet heart who is now happily married with a child. It was good seeing him and his family. It was also good to see another friend of mine who has been around on and off for over 14 years. He had a high school crush on me and apparently it's still there but for some reason we never actually got the chance to form a relationship. He has and is still a very nice and wonderful guy. Every time I see him we hang out but again never actually got the chance to see what life had to offer us together. I was on the move. The reunion was over and I was still hanging out with my friends and having fun. During this whole time I was too afraid to look back. I thought to myself man I have done so much damage I could not possibly turn back to my relationship with God. I felt like I was too much of a disappointment so I kept on going. Don't get me wrong I did enough just to say I prayed but nothing more. I wanted to but I just didn't know how. One day while I was at my parents' house sitting in the living room doing my school work (yes I am attending graduate school) I got a phone call from an old, old friend from way back in my elementary days. This young lady reminded me so much of me until it wasn't funny. Anyway we started talking and of course we get into the conversation about God. Tanika is her name, she started telling me how much things has changed in her life and how she couldn't see living without God. I was explaining to her how I felt the same way but I realized something and that was I felt somewhat comfortable with the way things were going in my life at the time. I wasn't sure if that was what I really meant but hey! At that time I was going with it. Tanika asked me about my book and if I was still going to have it out in a few months, I said well I huh! It was hard for me to answer that question. It was at that time. I knew I was confused about a few things and clearly one of them was my direction in life. Tanika was about two years younger than I was but she was very smart and goal oriented. She had already started a few businesses of her own along with giving back and helping the youth. Although we talked every once in a while it seemed like she always called just in the nick of time. After we got off the phone I continued to finish my school work before going to bed. I took in everything we talked about but it was still a few things left out there I had yet to realize. The following night I went out with my friends as usual and we had a really good time but I was somewhat still in between thought. The next night I stayed in the house, while sitting in the room I decided to take my thought and make it happen. I started talking to God again,

We'll God I am back, I know it seemed like forever but I guess I just didn't know how to face you after all this time. I don't know for some reason it seems like I just can't get it right. I guess maybe I just need to take it one day at a time instead of cramming several days into one. God the thing is I love you and I can't image what my life would be without you but sometimes I get scared. All my life you have been there even in the midst of my sins you seek to bless me daily. When I look back and see how far you have brought me and how you kept me I can't understand how I even though you would leave me. I can't believe I didn't think it was possible for me to turn back to the one who created me. God I am not perfect, every day I fall short of your glory but in the midst of it all, I keep going.

While praying I realized something, I had failed to realize and that was finding a balance. I never knew how to do both enjoy myself while maintaining my relationship with God. I have always found it easier to put more focus in friends and other people than in God and myself. I realized all that time and energy used to put in a friendship only 2% percent of that is given back. Don't get me wrong I appreciate my friends but my energy needed to take a turn in search of a balance in my life. It's funny because I was talking to a new found friend in my life (a young man) and one night he confirmed all of what I had already been praying about. It was really crazy how we met but crazy things happen to the best of us. I must admit I am very grateful for his insight and encouragement along the way.

The fun times were winding down and it was time for me to spend a little time in the house with my family. I am so blessed to have such a wonderful family. So many times we get caught up in friends and life itself until we forget about family. By this time I was taking a little break from friends and hanging out. I decided to redirect some attention toward family, myself, and my relationship with God. During this time I found out a lot of things I think I kinda knew but ignored. Anyway let's start with the exciting part, which was me spending time with my parents, brothers, sister-in-laws, nieces, and nephews. I had the chance to take my sister-in-law Madeca out for a sister's day and it was great. I treated her to a few things and it made me feel good to see the smile on her face. I tell you she has been such a blessing to my family especially to me. A sister, the feeling of having a real sister, what more could I ask for? I always knew that I was blessed with a wonderful family but this past summer made me realize it even more. I appreciate my sister-in-laws for giving birth to such wonderful children whom I have the great pleasure of being their aunt. My middle brother Dee also has a son and I am grateful for my nephew's mother giving birth to him. My fathers and brothers the men of my life I give thanks. To the Warrior of my being (mother) I give thanks. All of you have allowed me to grow and understand what it is like to have a family that loves you through thick and thin.

I had another week or two before it was time for me to return back to Maryland but of course I thought it would only be for a few more months. It's funny how things can change so suddenly. The original plan was for me and my friend Lee-lee to move to Atlanta Georgia around November, 2008. I mean we were telling everybody that was the plan and it was going to be a big move. Those plans never happened. I started thinking back to the times when I prayed asking God for an answer about making my move back down south. It dawned on me all this time I had been making plans to move but I never did get an answer or confirmation. All this time I wasn't thinking about nothing but what I wanted to do (which was move closer to home). Never once did I think that just maybe it wasn't my time yet and I still had some things to finish. I was blessed with a good job that allowed me to be off on holidays and summer months what more could I ask for at a time like this? Throughout the last week or so in South Carolina I spent time enjoying the fresh air, quietness, family, friends, and nature. I had a lot of time to think and search for a balance. My vacation in South Carolina was over and it was time for me to head back to my home in Maryland. On my ride back I started regaining focus and preparing myself for the completion of what I started which was my book. I not only wanted to finish what I started but appreciate the direction my life was going in, and reunite with my biological family as much as possible.

Step 11: The Pressure of the Process

Well I am sure you all have heard the saying be careful what you ask for, the last thing I remember saying was I just wanted to appreciate the direction my life was going in.

The pressure of the process, God at what point in my life do I become true to myself, at what point do I examined everything in my past that still affects me today? God you laid it on my heart to write, you purposely gave me the ideas, and gift to express words, of encouragement, strength, truth, inspiration, hurt, laughter, love, and direction, but again I ask myself at what point do I become true to myself and allow my experiences through this journey to lead me directly to you?

Growing up there was always some things you were taught to just keep it to yourself, and other things seemed somewhat alright to discuss. When I decided to write this book I thought I had covered everything in my past or at least the things I thought people needed to know without me feeling too ashamed, or better yet just enough of discussion about the things I had overcome. The entire time I have been writing saying this is supposed to be inspiration, motivation, and guidance for others; I still felt the need to be careful all because I didn't want to embarrass myself. Well I tell you what; God has his way of bringing it all to present. I have finally decided to accept his reason/purpose behind this book and that is for me to tell the truth even in the midst of my hurt and pain. I have to trust in God that he will cover and see me through it all.

Everyone has a secret, or a past time they never want to discuss. There are times when we feel like the hand we were given just isn't fair or better yet why can't my life just go according to the way I planned it. Well I am here to tell you, it doesn't work like that, yes for some the plan seems perfect and it happens just the way they wanted it, but as for me my plan was never my plan from the jump. I never had control, and all the while I thought I did but I really didn't. Yes I do believe we sometimes make choices or decisions to do certain things but at the same time the ultimate plan isn't ours. Take this walk with me as I enter into one of the hardest, deepest, challenges of my life thus far.

In August of 2008 I was faced with one of my deepest fears since childhood days, you know the one that was supposed to always remain a secret until death. I mentioned earlier on I grew up in a very religious household (a southern girl) and certain things just weren't supposed to happen. I can remember it like it was yesterday, I was about nine or ten years old, when I first touched another girl. It was my baby sitter; she was a little older than I was maybe by at least three to four years. Every now and then our parents would go out and she would watch me until they returned. A few times while watching me she would make me touch her. I don't remember exactly how many times this happen but I didn't know how I was supposed to feel. It was like I knew it was wrong but I didn't know what to do, after all she told me if I ever said anything I would be the one who got in trouble for it. I decided that this would be something I would take to my grave for two reasons: one is because I was ashamed of what people would think of me for allowing it to happen, and two I was scared and thought I would be the one to get in trouble for it. It's kind of hard to really determine if that was the leading factor of me having these feelings or if it was something that was already apart me? All I know is around that time I had these feelings, and I didn't understand it but I knew it was wrong. I spent a lot of time down on my knees at the alter praying asking God to please take that feeling (attraction) from me. I would pray the same prayer over and over again, every time I went to the alter thinking just maybe it would go away. I never discussed my darkest secret with anyone. Besides, it was something that just wasn't supposed to be and I thought I did a good job praying it away. Between the ages of nine and ten I experienced the touching of at least two other girls and after that I felt so bad and ashamed I never did it again, no matter how much I might have thought about it. Now that I think about it, it was actually a lot tougher than I thought but I did my best to suppress every thought that came to mind. I can even remember being in high school during basketball season, while in the locker room before practice or games. I wouldn't get dressed in the locker room. Instead I would go to the bathroom, not because I was ashamed of my body (I was only a buck thirty) but because I was afraid of something else that I just couldn't explain. Even when I got into college I would see other girls who weren't ashamed or afraid of their attraction toward other women, I somehow found myself to be cool with them just like I would with everyone else. But at the same time I always felt like I had to make it known that I wasn't interested in girls at all. I would ask them questions like how or what do you actually get out of being with another girl? I always made sure they knew I didn't have a problem with what they did and to me it never changed who they were or made me look at them any different. I would always say things like I love me some men no doubt, don't thing I could ever see myself with a girl. Around the same time I decided to cut my hair and grow dreads, it was something I wanted to do for a while but was afraid. Finally

I decided to go through with it and my biological sister who never seemed to have anything nice to say made a comment to my brother (oh I see your sister is growing dreads so what is she gay)? When I found that out I was hurt deeply, I cried and told my mother that raised me I can't see why she would say such a thing like that about me?

Well anyway for a while things just started to kind of fade and I was having sex, dating, and having fun. The crazy thing is although during high school I got dressed in the bathroom at times, and asked questions here and there to my friends in college I knew was attracted to women. Although I cried and felt so hurt when my sister called me gay when I cut my hair, I still totally dismissed how any of this could play apart in me possibly still having those feelings (attraction) toward girls because again I thought I prayed it away. Well I guess I didn't do such a good job because it all came back to me at the age of twenty eight four months before my twenty ninth birthday, I had discovered something about myself that again I had only tried to suppress since I was a child and that was my attraction for women.

Toward the end of August, 2008 I had my first real experience with a woman; it wasn't something I planned more like something that just happened. I didn't know what to do or think almost like the first time when my baby sitter made me touch her only this time, I was older, and it was more than just a touch. At that moment I checked out of life and as soon as I could I got away from her thinking I played it safe but that was just the beginning. I had quickly developed some type of feelings and emotions I could not explain and I cried for days and nights at a time. I didn't understand what was happening to me and I refused to talk to anyone because I was so ashamed. Finally I met this other young lady who basically came to my rescue in a way. You see she had experienced something very similar to me about a year prior to my experience so she was able to help me cope with my situation and before I knew it we had started dealing with one another. It started out being just for fun, for some odd reason I felt like as long as I was doing it just for fun or as long as it was a third party male involved it was okay; truth is I was in serious denial. Before I knew it I had fallen for her. It wasn't just for fun anymore it actually turned into a real relationship and it was at that point when my struggle for so many years (I thought I put to rest) came to realization. I didn't understand what it meant, didn't know what others or my family would think of me. I thought to myself there is no way God could ever still love me. I had experienced a level of emotions, connection, and commitment that I had only been longing for as long as I could remember. I know that sounds like some awesome news but it was hard to swallow when the person I finally got that connection with happen to be another woman.

I was struggling daily with myself, my sexuality, and my relationship with God. I thought I really did it this time, there was no way I could turn back to God because this was just too much for me. I felt like I had let him down to a point of no return. Time continued to go on and it had been well over a year, my feelings only grew stronger and because I was in love and ashamed I had lost myself, and although I had finally experienced love it was still incomplete. I battled, I beat myself up, and I was ashamed of being attracted to a woman. I was worried about what others and especially my family would think of me, stuck in the religious way of thinking which only caused me to stop all connection with God. I mean I would attempt to pray but my heart, mind, body, and soul was gone. I had walked away from the one who carried me all my life, I had stopped calling home as much, going home, and reaching out to anyone who I thought would be disappointed in me. My ability to inspire, strengthen, help, or motivate others was at a standstill, because mentally I couldn't even help myself. I had stopped writing, reading, thinking, and even sleeping. I was so caught up in being afraid, disappointed, and in love until I had totally forgotten how to love myself. I beat myself up so badly; and I had gotten to a place where I just wanted to end my life. It seemed easier that way. It wasn't because I experienced love that had me feeling this way but it was whom I experienced it with. So the entire time I spent hiding, trying to explain my feelings but nothing came out of it, I was caught up in being in love, upset about who I was in love with, and mad with myself for allowing this to happen. I even tried to talk with my mother, explaining these feelings I was having but she quickly pulled out the bible, told me she didn't want her experience with my father to be the reason why I was feeling this way. Well I found myself shutting down on her instantly and after that I thought this is it, I am all alone. There was no way I could face my family, or that they would understand what I was going through. I spent more nights crying than anything, I felt all alone and no matter how hard it was, I didn't turn back to God and that only made things even more complicated.

After a year and a few months I started trying to piece things together, I even went back into my childhood days just so I could try to find some level of understanding. I decided to write this letter to myself but it was more of me tapping into my past and inner feelings.

Dear Self:

For some reason I always found it easy to hang around women. My personality and my ability to portray both a dominant and a feminine side often attracted both sexes. Ever since I can remember or should I say started dating guys it was always something missing. Most of the time I enjoyed the friendship more than I enjoyed anything else, commitment was something I was afraid of. I didn't want to think of the idea of just being with one guy or the fact that we would have to actually have sex often. I started having sex when I was like twenty years old, late bloomer. I dated here and there nothing serious. I never really had anything too serious outside of high school and even then it wasn't serious. I don't know but for some reason I always felt incomplete, all I knew was marriage and kids was the way I was supposed to go. Anyway as I got older and moved away from home I found myself dealing with different guys but it was never anything outside of sex and goodbyes, or just maybe a long lasting friendship. I love you was never in my vocabulary, relationships didn't fit well, connection; I never had. So I was still searching for what I was missing. I gave men a hard time without them even knowing it; I don't know I often think it has a lot to do with my upbringing. You see my father cheated on my mother constantly, still until this day she deals with him cheating every now and again. My father did drugs at one point in his life, during that time he would put his hands on my mother. Countless nights I couldn't sleep too afraid of what he might do to her…result in me fearing for her life and hurting for mine. Forgetting it is not an option, forgiving I can see but I lost so much respect for my father until it's almost too late and too hard to gain it back. I love him yes; I mean he was the man I looked up too. I was a daddy's little girl but I guess after a while it faded into one big dream for me. My brother on the other hand followed in my father's footsteps with cheating. As his sister I watched and helped him keep it going so I grew up knowing all the tricks of the trade. Somewhere along the way I managed to have it all backwards. You see I treat women like I always wanted to see my father and brother treat women and I treat men as if it was some type of payback, basically the way I saw them treat women. Don't get me wrong I respect men but my tolerance is very low and for some reason I struggle with being in a relationship with them. I am very strong, independent, and tough. Watching my mother I gained so much strength and independence. One thing my brothers and father taught me was never to depend on anyone for anything and although they managed to cheat here and there they were great men, providers, and great fathers. So here I am mixed all into one, very independent, caring, nurturing, loving, helpful, but when it comes to men I have a guard up and for some reason I have never been able to form a deep connection. I mean I loved him, but there is a difference between loving and being in love and clearly I wasn't in love with him. Loving him wasn't hard, I was able to maintain and do the things women and or a wife would do in a relationship but something stopped me from having that deep connection with him. I struggled with letting my guard down, I struggled with letting go of my independence, I struggled with accepting authority from him, and I struggled with commitment. I struggled with being able to fall in love with him, and that was a big problem. I enjoyed our time together. He was a great friend, but the question still remained will I ever be able to form that connection, and commitment? I don't know all of this just seemed so crazy, especially coming from such a religious back ground as mine. Some things just aren't supposed to happen you know? It had gotten so bad until I felt like I would never fall in love almost at a point where I didn't really believe in love. For so many years I thought falling in love would never live in me. I would just live the rest of my life as if love didn't really exist. All of a sudden it happened. I experienced multiple feelings, emotions, and connections. I finally knew what it felt like to commit, to be vulnerable, to let down your guard, to release levels of independency, and embrace every moment of it. For the first time in my 29 years of living I had finally knew what it was like to be in love. I had allowed myself to open up and I couldn't understand how something that is said to be so wrong, feel so right. Although I felt free, I still battled with myself, religion, God, society, fear, and my sexuality. I am at war with myself because I didn't understand what was happening to me. I didn't understand why I was able to have such feelings and connection with another woman. I am scared because after all these years of hiding I had finally discovered this part of me. The part I ran from since my childhood days. I started to question myself, and when I factor in religion, God, my family, and society the fear really kicked in and I began to isolate myself. I was experiencing a real disconnection. Growing up the religious way tells me to go find a husband; same sex is a sin, abomination for that matter, a curse, basically a first class pass to hell. Because of the religious way of thinking there was no way God could ever forgive me or love me anymore. I am afraid to turn God's way, I was ashamed of myself and every day I struggle with wondering what will my family think of me? Will they still love me the same? Will I lose my family? This was by far the hardest thing ever, feeling like I let God and my family down. This would all be easier if I just killed myself, this way I wouldn't have to worry about letting God, or my family down. I could escape society and its views on homosexuality; I could just do away with facing people. I could escape this cruel world and the judgment it places on the lives of many. I could go and free myself of all aspects of life. So here I am trying to find my way, trying to figure out where I stand with God, religion, society, and my sexuality. This is very hard for me, I am hurting unconditionally; I don't know where to turn, what to do, or how to get out. Most of my friends express major concern about me daily because I am so isolated. Some of them couldn't seem to understand it, while others held my hand every step of the way even though I wasn't being completed honest with them. The truth is I don't know how to be honest with myself. So this is why I decided to write this letter, because I am searching for honesty, closure, freedom, happiness and love within myself. I am crying out but it seems like no one can hear my cry. I had just turned thirty years old and instead of that being a joyful time it was more of a confusing time. I was more confused than ever. I felt like I was hitting rock bottom and something had to be done. It was time for me to do what I know is right in my soul because my heart wasn't strong enough to make any decisions. So finally I started trying to go back to church but it was hard. It seemed like every message made me feel guilty. I tried to read my bible but I just could not get anywhere. I had beaten myself up so bad until it was just too hard to face God. I didn't have any strength to do anything. After I had lost myself and I stop loving myself I was tapped out. I had started depending on my ability to be in love to make me feel like I loved myself, I had finally experienced what is was like to be in a relationship, to depend on someone else, to be depended on, to feel good, or just the idea of being able to spend time with that person. It was like the best feeling and the worst feeling all at the same time. I struggled with myself and what I wanted. It was at that moment I realized that I had given up my whole heart to being in love and I had somehow started to fall out of love, out of touch with God.

It was the struggle, hurt, and pain of losing who I was that brought me back to God; it was the struggled from feeling like no one understood what I was going through, the pain from missing my family, heartache from disappointment within myself, and heartache from feeling like I had lost touch with God. It was nothing I could do on my own to fix this pain and at that moment I knew my only help was God. So I started trying to take one day at a time reaching back out to God. I spent nights, days, moments, and seconds crying from all the pain I felt inside. It took everything out of me to smile, and even then it wasn't a real smile. I was in so much pain, and although I had so many wonderful friends around me that kept encouraging me, nothing they said really made a difference at that moment. I prayed, and I prayed, and I cried but nothing was happening. I went to church but after the message was over I was right back where I started from. For about two weeks every time I tried to pray, I cried, and every time I cried it wasn't a cry for God. I was weak, and my heart was on fire, my mind was constantly battling with my sexuality being in love and feeling convicted. I thought this could all have been prevented or could be easier if I would just give up now and conform to the way of society, the way of what my family would want, and to the religious side of life. At least if I do it the conformed way, God would love and accept me again.

Well I continued to make prayer attempts, and attend church but it was like God wasn't responding and I could not feel his presence no matter how much I tried, I guess it was because I wasn't trying hard enough. I had purchased a book written by TD Jakes entitled strength for every moment. It was like a daily inspirational piece, I started reading it every day and spending more time alone (something I had not done in a very long time). No matter how I felt I made sure I took the time to read, pray, and spend time alone. I even started back reading another one of my favorite books, The Purpose Driven Life. I was determined to gain a relationship/friendship with God but of course I was still running into the same obstacles of battling with my sexuality, loving myself again, and giving my heart back to God. On July 25th, 2010 Sunday morning I had just finished reading T.D. Jakes inspirational day fifteen topic: Be transformed.

I can remember reading this passage that stated: And do not be conformed to this world, but be transformed by the renewing of your mind, that you may prove what is that good and acceptable and perfect will of God (Romans 12.2). After reading this passage I began to pray, by this time I felt angry and upset. I was tired of feeling like God didn't hear my cry. I was upset because I was tired of the pain. I was tired of feeling so convicted. I was tired of running. I was tired of feeling like every time I try to move forward with my relationship with God It felt like nothing was happening. I was angry because here I am battling with homosexuality, when I didn't ask for this. I just wanted to be normal and live a normal conformed life. I was so tired of hurting, and feeling like I was in bondage with no way out, so I prayed this prayer of complete honesty and truth:

"God, I am sorry, please forgive me. I confess I can't live without you. I am nothing without you, I am sorry for turning my back on you. I want to have a relationship, friendship with you. I need you to take my heart back. God I confess I battle with my sexuality, I battle with loving, serving you, and feeling convicted. I don't know what to do. I tried to pray having these feelings for women away, but it is here and even in the midst I still want nothing more than to serve and love you without feeling so horrible. I want to be free. I want to love myself again. God please talk to me I don't know what to do. God please take back my heart, mind, and soul and renew all of me. I don't know what to do. I just need to know that you will always love me no matter what. I feel like this is a part of me I can't change but I am about to lose my mind, so please God help me, guide me, strengthen me again, I have come to you poring my heart out; I don't know what else you want me to do. Yes I am angry because I feel like you're not hearing me, like you're not helping me, God yes I trust in you, I believe in you, I have faith in you, so God I know you're going to see me through". I have nothing else left in me so please help me. I am afraid of what others, my family, religious leaders, and society will think of me. I am afraid my family will be disappointed in me. I am afraid because according to the bible homosexuality is a sin but God what am I supposed to do? Where do I go from here?

This was the first time I had ever went to this extreme in prayer with God, it was like I had poured everything in me out, and although he knows all about me and my every move, I still felt the need to confess and be honest with him, I felt like this was the only way I was going to be free, this was the only way I was going to find peace, happiness, love again for myself, guidance, strength, and some type of renewing within my heart, mind, and soul. After I finish praying I went on about my day. The funny thing is a week before this day I prayed asking God to help me and give me confirmation by the end of that week. Of course nothing happened. So when I finished praying this time, I still felt like nothing happened but I didn't let it stop me from talking to God and reading. The thing is I had already started to receive a little strength here and there, and I could feel a little difference in my mind, heart, and soul but it wasn't enough to pull me through everything I had been going through for the last two years. It wasn't enough to make me feel alright with myself and my sexuality while still trying to serve God. After I finished praying I started reading The Purpose Driven Life, it was at least five chapters that stood out to me the most and those were The Heart of Worship, Becoming Best Friends with God, Developing a friendship with God, "Worship That please God", and When God seem Distant. It was crazy because right after I finished praying I read the chapter " Developing a friendship with God" In this chapter Rick Warren touched on a few things that made perfect sense such as: The truth is you are as close to God as you choose to be. Intimate friendship with God is a choice, not an accident. You must intentionally seek it. He also mention how a person may have been passionate with God but lost the desire, he mention people doing things out of duty instead of love, if you have just been going through the motions spiritually don't be surprised when God allows pain in your life. Pain is the fuel of passion-it energizes us with intensity to change that we don't normally possess, your problems are not punishment just wake-up calls from a loving God. God is not mad at you, he is mad about you and he will do what it takes to bring you back to fellowship with him. Then in the Chapter "Worship that pleases God" Rick Warren said: you don't bring glory to God by trying to be someone he never intended you to be. God wants you to be yourself. Of course the next chapter "When God seem Distant" hit it right on the head.

Rick Warren said: How do you praise God when you don't understand what's happening in your life and God is silent? How do you stay connected in a crisis without communication? How do you keep your eyes on Jesus when they're full of tears? You pour out your heart to God. Unload every emotion that you're feeling.

Understand something; I am not here to justify sin in anyway. I am not here to speak against religion or leaders within ministries but I am here trying to find peace within myself, a level of comfort, truth, and strength to go forward. Through life my experiences, especially battling with my sexuality has humbled my soul, changed my life, increased my love for God, and allowed me to appreciate my family and friends more than ever. I am learning how to depend on God, family, and friends more than thinking I can do it all by myself. I can truly say God has taught me how to value love, relationships, and honesty. I take every message preached, and every word written, and use it to strengthen me, so that I can provide strength to others, and support system, and guidance. You see I was one of those Christians going through the motions (out of duty). Maybe it was because I was raised in church so everything became like a ritual to me. I knew how to praise him, how to run around the church, when to sit down and when to stand up but when it was time for the word I was ready to take a nap. I had a passion but lost my desire. I was conformed to the way every leader of the church preached. Everything that went on in church somehow had an impact on me and my relationship with God. I found myself judging others not in church like me but again God has his way of bringing pain and hurt not to destroy his people but to strengthen and open their eyes. I realized that God isn't mad at me but he is mad about me and at the end of the day it's not about the members in the church, what they do or how they do it but it's about me developing my own relationship with God. So when I go to church now I run only if I feel the need, I sit when I am ready I listen to every word and use it for my good to gain God's glory. I decided that even in the midst of everything going on in my life I will not run or hide from God or anyone else. I will never judge another person or frown upon anyone, even when leaders touch home and speak about homosexuality I will not let that run me out of church. I will read my bible and continue to pray because I am a believer that God has his hands on me and my life is a living testimony. I realize that homosexuality doesn't make me who I am, and it doesn't change my character. I will always be that fun, loving, honest, loyal, friendly, caring, and happy person whose desire is to make a difference in the lives of others, to help, encourage, and strengthen. To make them laugh, to hold them when they cry, and give to them when they are in need.

I pray:

I pray this prayer, I pray that man will look, listen, and think before speaking against another person. I pray to all ministers, and religious leaders, remember why God has called you to lead. Remember where you started and even where you are currently. No man is perfect but every man lives in imperfection. Judge not your brother or sister but help them. I know so many people young and old who have strayed away from church for several reasons, homosexuality, addiction, domestic abuse, the list goes on but you see our leaders need a wakeup call. Time is running out and the imperfect people they are letting slip away. Some leaders are too busy living a lie of their own, while others are preaching perfection in my imperfection. There are people like me who sit on the fence, meaning I want nothing more than to serve God. Church is my home, so while I sit on this fence please don't knock me over the edge instead help me. My life is a living testimony. Pain plus hurt keeps me loving, trusting, and fighting for God more and more every day. My life and everything in it isn't an accident. I pray to religious leaders and sometime religious family members and friends who frowned upon certain sins and not all. I pray that you guys will wake up, stop pointing fingers, pulling out bible verses but listen, help, guide, and unconditionally love that son, that daughter, granddaughter, who come to you and express feelings, thoughts, concerns, with their sexuality, relationships, situations, whatever it may be. Please listen, too many people (young children) even older adults like myself who know about religion, who hate to disappoint family, who worry about society's way of thinking often feel like ending life or suppressing through is better than not being excepted or understood especially by those you love the most. I know it sounds crazy because here I am thirty years old going through such a situation but it happens. I pray that Gods love, grace, and mercy will forever be upon me and through his love I won't ever have to run from him again but embrace myself, who I am, who I am becoming, and who God has called me to be. I pray that even in my moments of fear, doubt, pain, hurt, and lack of understanding God will continue to strengthen me. I pray that my soul will continue to humble itself through this term call life and in eternity I will live accordingly to Gods glory. As long as I am here on earth I will not be conformed to judgment of man but when I reach eternity it is at that time God will be the judge of my life as he knows my heart. Every day I fall short of Gods glory and I know that I am not perfect but I am blessed to know that God loves me no matter what. It is a blessing to be given one day at a time and I will cherish each day with thanks as if it was my last. My girl Vickie Winans said it best in her song (Stand up and Carry On) I know that the race is not given to the swift but to those who endure to the end.

Amen.

I decided to reach out once more to my family. It was very hard for me but it was something I had to do. I remember it like it was yesterday, I was riding home from a friend's house and all of a sudden I felt the urge to call my mother. This wasn't a normal since of urgency, more like I needed to settle my spirit.

I was finally coming into a place of comfort and acceptance and it was time I expressed myself to my family, especially my mother.

Mother/Daughter Conversation: Ring, Ring, Ring, Hello, said my mother. Hi Mom I said, how was your day? It was pretty good said my mother is everything alright? Umm! Yes ma'am (tears began to roll down my face, I realize I could no longer hold it in) ma, I said I need to tell you something, yes dear (it was almost like she already knew what I wanted to say, like she had been waiting on this moment for a while now). I stuttered for about two minutes then starting crying, ma you know I have been battling with something for a while and I just had to come to you. I know you notice that I have been very distant from the family, and almost felt like never reaching out to you all again but…but what she said, talk to me. Well ma I have been battling with my sexuality for a while now, I have been down and out, depressed, and basically almost to a point of ending my life. I thought you guys would not accept me, especially since that time I tried to talk about it with you and you pulled out the bible on me. You said you didn't want me to feel this way because of what you and daddy went through, but truth is ma, it's deeper than that. I have an attraction for women, I seem to have a connection and sense of happiness with them that I have never felt before. It's hard because I still find men attractive but emotionally, my connection to women lies deep within and it is something I just can't explain. Can you try to explain it sweetie my mother said, well it's like for so many years I dated men and it was cool but I always felt incomplete, never settled, or even happy for that matter. I found it so much easier to be good friends with them, and again it's not that I don't find them attractive it's just that I have no connection, no desire, no level of commitment to them. As the tears rolled down my face, I said ma I just didn't think you guys would love me anymore because of this. Sweetie said my mother, how could you ever think such a thing, she said I knew this was what you were dealing with. She said God laid it on my heart a while ago and I knew when you were ready you would come to me. She said baby, I will love you always unconditionally for the rest of my life. Who you prefer does not change my love for you, nor does it define who you are as a person. She said I will always love you and whomever you chose just as much as I love you. She said you were a gift to me (one of the greatest) and I would never stop loving you just because you prefer to be with a woman. She said the only thing that matters is no matter what you do keep God first in your life, no matter which you choose make sure they have a relationship with God. She said both women and men can hurt you and let you down, we are all human but God will guide you accordingly. She said seek God for understanding and listen to what he says and I promise you everything will be alright. Tears continued to roll down my face; it was at that moment I realize my mother's unconditional love was true, it was at that moment my relationship with my mother grew stronger than before, it was at that moment I remembered the importance of family, it was at that moment my life changed forever. It felt like a burden I had been carrying for years was lifted and I was finally set free. I am grateful for family. I have learned the importance of forgiveness and unconditional love.

    Writing this book and opening my heart to God allowed me to face challenges, forgive, love unconditionally, and develop new relationships with biological family (especially with my biological father) and move forward after over thirty years. During these 30 plus years I spent so much time blaming God and other people for what happened in my life. The time I didn't spend pointing fingers I was so busy trying to make everyone else happy until I forgot about myself, my family, and God. One of the hardest things in life is trying to be someone else other than who God created you to be. I found out that some of my problems in life I create on my own, most of my struggles can be overcome, and different seasons has different reasons. I am currently in a place where finding my purpose is a must, through my findings I am also in search of a balance in God and my life. I don't know where or what's next but I do know that my life is a living testimony. Never in a million years did I think I would be ending this book with the whole truth. Never did I think that I would be one to live such a sensitive subject call homosexuality. This book doesn't make situations in life easier nor does it make certain things that happen in life right but it does provide hope, truth, inspiration, motivation, and faith. We have the option of making changes in our lives taking us steps closer to God, happiness, peace, love, forgiveness, success, and whatever else our heart desires. As for me I am in search of all the above especially for my purpose and commitment to God. I am learning from my past; using it to help me live in the present, while preparing for the future. **The Pressure of the Process Continues…….**

Special Tribute (Sister-in-laws & Brothers)

Stand-up, be strong was what you said
Focus pay close attention
Forget about negative words mention

Giving birth to wonderful children
Who became my nieces and nephews
Smart enough to strive
Powerful enough to hide their pride

Going to college
Gaining self-knowledge is what I imagine
Keeping God first and never giving up
Even when the struggle gets tuff

The smile on their faces
Makes me work harder in paving the way
The funny things they do
Keeps me loving you

Knowing no other person
Could ever fill your shoes
Keeps me at ease

The thought of the world being so corrupted
Keeps me praying each day
That my nieces and nephews
Hold tight and stay strong
Allowing me to again pave the way
Through corruption in society today

I am sure without you
It would be no them
Meaning no one to strive as hard as "I"
Let's cut to the chase
No other can ever take your place

"Love overrides" (biological family)

Over the years the pain grew strong
Wanting to blame each of you for what went wrong

30 years of running from what's to gain
God finally allows me to endure the pain

Reaching out for deliverance
Forgiveness among us all
Praying that we will survive the fall

Set out in different directions
Only to find our destination
Purposely design
God's gift to man kind
Therapy to my soul
Peace within in my heart
All these years I was made to be set apart

Finally I surrender
Free from bondage
No more will I hide what I feel inside
All is forgiven and love overrides

Made in the USA
Charleston, SC
09 February 2014